ASSASSINATION
*A Special
Kind of Murder*

Books by Willard Heaps

THE BRAVEST TEENAGE YANKS
THE WALL OF SHAME
RIOTS, U.S.A.
THE STORY OF ELLIS ISLAND
WANDERING WORKERS
BIRTHSTONES
ASSASSINATION: *A Special Kind of Murder*

WILLARD A. HEAPS

ASSASSINATION
A Special Kind of Murder

Meredith Press   New York

COPYRIGHT © 1969 BY WILLARD A. HEAPS

All rights reserved. No part of this book in excess of five hundred words may be reproduced in any form without permission in writing from the publisher.

First edition

SBN: 696-52038-9
Library of Congress Catalog Card Number: 73-93835
MANUFACTURED IN THE UNITED STATES OF AMERICA
FOR MEREDITH PRESS

8819

CONTENTS

1. MURDER FOR A CAUSE	3
2. ASSASSINS AND THEIR PLOTS	20
3. TWO BIBLICAL ASSASSINATIONS	36
4. DAGGERS AND SWORDS IN ANCIENT ROME	43
5. MURDER IN A CATHEDRAL	49
6. A CRUSADER-VICTIM OF THE HASHASHEEN	56
7. A LEADER OF THE FRENCH REVOLUTION	60
8. THE FUSE OF WORLD WAR I: SARAJEVO	66
9. VICTIMS OF THE RUSSIAN REVOLUTION	73
10. VIOLENT DEATH OF A NONVIOLENT LEADER	89
11. THE MIDDLE EAST	95

12.	THE FAR EAST AND SOUTHERN ASIA	116
13.	LATIN AMERICA AND THE CARIBBEAN	131
14.	KILLERS IN THE NEW AFRICA	156
15.	GUNS IN THE UNITED STATES	169
	APPENDIX:	201
	OTHER MAJOR ASSASSINATIONS	203
	SELECTED READING	207
	INDEX	214

ASSASSINATION
A Special Kind of Murder

chapter one

MURDER FOR A CAUSE

The figure takes aim, a leader falls, and an assassin has done his work—for overthrow of a government, for vengeance, for patriotism, for imagined wrongs, for fame, for any number of reasons.

The roll call of those who have died by the hands of assassins is as long as history. Twenty of Rome's emperors were slain. In twelve centuries of Irish history from A.D. 4 to 1172, thirty-one of seventy-eight kings were murdered. Japanese history is filled with political assassinations, usually by the sword. During the Italian Renaissance Machiavelli proclaimed that the end justified the means, and the Borgias used stilettos and poison to eliminate political enemies.

Successful assassinations and unsuccessful attempts are facts of life today. During the ten months spent in researching and writing this book, from April, 1968, to January, 1969, seven prominent figures were murdered—Martin Luther King in April, Senator Robert F. Kennedy in June, and U.S. Ambassador to Guatemala John Mein, in August; the ex-president of Lebanon in May; a judge and provincial governor in the Philippines in July; and the Education Minister of South Vietnam in January. At least four attempts were made—the President of Aden's Ruling Council in July, Greek Premier George Papadapoulos in August, Pakistan President Mohammed Ayub Khan in November, and Emperor Hirohito of Japan in January. The number of plots which have been uncovered during that period is impossible to estimate because most countries do not reveal such information.

European history is blood-saturated with assassination. Czars, kings, and emperors, queens and empresses, premiers, foreign ministers, and cabinet ministers have been murdered. Two Presidents of the French Republic have been killed, and the list for other countries is extensive. Many Latin American dictators and political leaders have been felled by guns and knives. Middle Eastern figures have been shot and bombed. The United States' record is shocking.

Just what is assassination and why is it "a special kind of murder"? What makes this distinction? First, it might be well to examine the definitions of the verb "assassinate" in a few dictionaries and encyclopedias:

Webster's New International Dictionary, 3d edition
1. To murder by sudden or secret attack.
2. To injure or destroy unexpectedly and treacherously.

Random House Dictionary of the English Language
1. To kill suddenly or secretly.

New International Encyclopedia
The act of taking the life of anyone by surprise or treacherous violence, either by a hired emissary, as in the case of political plots, or by a fanatic who hopes to further his ideas through the death of his victim. Generally the term is applied to the murder of a public personage by one who aims solely at the death of the victim.

The English word "assassin" is a transliteration of the Arabic word *hashasheen,* meaning "drinkers of hashish," a narcotic drug derived from hemp that is chewed, smoked, or drunk for its intoxicating effect. Hashasheen was the term applied to the members of a secret Ismaili fraternity that flourished in northern Persia, Iraq, and Syria from 1090 to 1256. Its founder was Hasan ibn-al-Sabbah, better known as the Old Man of the Mountain, who seized the mountain of Alamut in northern Persia, and from that stronghold ten thousand feet above the sea waged a campaign of terror and murder against the opponents and persecutors of the Ismaili faith. The fraternity had several degrees of initiation, the lowest members of which, generally young men, were required to obey absolutely any of their leader's commands.

The candidates for admission to the order were given hashish to drink; when stupefied by it, they were brought into a beautiful garden, and on recovering their senses they were told they were in paradise. After four or five days of wine, women, and good food, they were again drugged with hashish and were carried from the garden. Upon waking, they invariably asked for the lost paradise and were told that they would be readmitted to it, and forever, if they would obey the master faithfully or be slain in his service. Those who complied were the *hashasheen*. For almost two centuries they seized the castles of their enemies and conducted a campaign of terrorism. Murder was the instrument of their policy. Their principal targets were their bitter enemies, the Muslims, and they also attacked the Crusaders who invaded their realm, their most prominent victim being Conrad of Montferrat. The order declined and was almost nonexistent by 1256.

The occurrence of assassinations has varied in different periods and localities. In times of internal strife and political upheaval, when emotions reach a high peak, a wave of murders is apt to occur, and their number and brutality follow a common pattern. When national peace is restored, assassination is no longer so prevalent.

Russia under both the Czarist and Communist regimes has been the most assassination-prone of all countries. The long period of absolute royal rule, with the almost unparalleled power of the nobility contrasted with the continuous oppressive serfdom of the peasants, was marked by tides of violence and murder. Anarchists in pre-Communist days made public figures the constant targets of assassins. Anarchism was suppressed by the Communists after the 1917 Revolution and the fall of the Romanov dynasty, but from 1878 to 1911, one Czar, at least four ministers, three prominent army generals, four provincial governors of the nobility, and several princes, dukes, and counts were assassinated.

Assassination attempts and a few successful political murders have continued under Communist rule since the 1917 revolution. Though seldom publicized or even officially denied, information has occasionally leaked to the outside world. Two attempts were made on the life of Vladimir Lenin in 1918. Under Stalin the most important political murder was the assassination of Sergei Kirov, Communist leader and one of Stalin's closest friends, in 1934, which led to treason trials and party purges. No attempts on Stalin's life were officially reported, but some Russians contend that such attempts were made, leading to his reluctance to appear in public. Two attempts to assassinate Nikita Khrushchev, in 1962 and 1964, have been reported, but both have been officially denied.

What has been assumed outside of the Soviet Union to be an attempt on the lives of Leonid Brezhnev, leader of the Communist Party, and President Nikolai Podgorny, occurred on January 22, 1969, during a Moscow ceremonial procession carrying Soviet cosmonauts and officials to a mass meeting. The four most recent cosmonauts were standing in the first automobile, some of the earlier cosmonauts were riding in the second, and a number of prominent officials were in cars following. At the entrance of the Kremlin a figure stepped out of the crowd and opened fire at the second car, killing the chauffeur and wounding a motorcycle outrider, apparently assuming that top Kremlin leaders were riding in it. Aside from revealing that the assailant was an army deserter wearing a blue-coated police uniform, officials have imposed a tight clamp of secrecy. The immediate result, however, is that party leaders riding in official cars on Moscow streets are now accompanied by both advance and follow-up automobiles as well as motorcycle escorts.

Japan has also been in the forefront among nations, a close second to Russia, where political assassination has been concerned. Nine premiers have been murdered since 1860, four of these since the end of World War I. The tradition of murder for the good of the nation has been followed continuously, and the emergence of the country as a world power with developing democratic institutions has been met with violent opposition, often of a terrorist nature.

Certainly vying for a place in any list of assassination-prone countries are the states of southeastern Europe grouped under the term Balkans. These were particularly active in the turbulent period following World War I when nationalist feelings were at their peak and new country boundaries resulted in minorities of substantial sizes.

In Bulgaria, for example, following an internal struggle, Prime Minister Aleksandr STAMBOLISKI, founder of the Agrarian Party and often called the Peasant Statesman, was assassinated in a *coup d'etat* on June 8, 1923. While all his ministers were being arrested in their homes, Stamboliski, pursued to his native village by an armed detachment, fled across the mountains, hoping to reach the frontier, but was overtaken and shot on June 14. The succeeding head of government, Todor ALEKSANDROV, was murdered in the next year on August 31, 1924. During that year alone there were about two hundred assassinations of Bulgarian government and opposition leaders. In 1925 an attempt was made on the life of King Boris, and General Kosta GEORGIEV was killed the next day. Other Balkan states were caught up in this foment of opposition, mainly by nationalists, and political murders were commonplace. The Sarajevo murder was probably the one assassination in all history, ancient and modern, which caused the greatest worldwide repercussions.

The record of the United States is almost unequaled for the assassinations of its heads of state. Four presidents have been murdered while in office, at least five unsuccessful attempts have been made, and scores of plots have been uncovered before they could be put into action. In contrast to the experience of most other nations, in the United States high government officials such as Cabinet members have escaped death. United States foreign-service officers have rarely been murdered in spite of the fact that many American consulates and embassies have been attacked during the upheavals in various countries. One of these victims was Thomas WASSON, a consul general, who was shot by a sniper in Jerusalem in 1948 during the Palestine war. The other was John G. MEIN, American ambassador to Guatemala, in 1968.

Some countries have been relatively free from political murder. Canada, a comparatively new nation, has had only one major assassination, that of Darcy McGEE, member of Parliament. Two other Parliament members—John S. Sheridan and George Brown—have been murdered, but their violent deaths had no political purpose and may therefore be labeled as murders rather than assassinations.

Great Britain is another example of a nation which has been relatively free from political murders. Although its long history is filled with murders in the struggles for power, only three assassinations of major figures have taken place: Prime Minister Spencer PERCEVAL in 1812; and Lord Frederick CAVENDISH, Chief Secretary for Ireland, and Under-Secretary for Ireland Thomas BURKE in Dublin by members of a Fenian society in 1882. However, when Britain's colonial empire extended throughout the world, representatives of the Crown were frequently assassinated, usually by fanatics or nationalists. Almost two dozen men of prominence, serving in various colonial posts, were thus murdered during the latter part of the nineteenth century. The most prominent of such figures was Lord MOYNE, British Minister of State in the Middle East, in 1944.

The distinction between murder and assassination is most simply exemplified by power struggles within royal families throughout history. A reigning monarch almost inevitably encountered opposition from brothers, sisters, and other relatives, who yearned for the throne. Succession as the birthright of an individual was challenged both from the standpoint of personality and inheritance. Pretenders or usurpers as well as kings frequently became murder victims. Internal plots found members of the same family pitted against each other. When the purpose was to eliminate a king for such personal reasons, the killing was a murder rather than an assassination.

The assassination of a king, or regicide, is often the result of a conspiracy against the reigning monarch. The assassinations of many English Kings, for example, were plotted and planned by enemies of the royal family, jealous officials and advisers, or groups of nobles out of favor with the family in power or eager to resort to murder in order to place a favorite candidate on the throne. Several such murders occurred during the Wars of the Roses, 1455 to 1485, which was a struggle between the noble houses of Lancaster and York. The well-known, and still controversial, disposition of thirteen-year-old Edward V and his younger brother Richard during their imprisonment in the Tower of London in 1483 on the orders of their uncle Richard, Duke of Gloucester, who thus became Richard III, is a tragic story. The fate of the two children in the Tower of London is still a mystery, though the most natural assumption is that their uncle ordered their deaths. Skeletons, presumed to be those of the princes, were unearthed in the Tower during the reign of Charles II almost two centuries later.

Another example of the difficult distinction between murder and assassination is found in the deaths of three figures close to Mary Stuart, Queen of Scots—David Rizzio, her sercretary, in 1566; Lord Darnley, her second husband and cousin, the next year; and the Earl of MORAY, her half brother in 1570. The first two are clearly murders, the other assassination. The Italian Rizzio became her favorite, and the reliance Mary placed in him caused jealousy and hatred on the part of many great nobles. They persuaded Darnley that Rizzio was her lover, and with his support broke into Holyrood Palace, seized the offender in Mary's presence, and stabbed him over fifty times. The plot to kill Darnley was even more vicious. On the night of February 9, 1567, his house was blown up by gunpowder. In the morning the bodies of Darnley and his page were found strangled in the garden. Moray, who had been involved in both of these plots and had always worked against her interests, was murdered in 1570 by a band of lords. Since he was a leading political figure who, the lords evidently believed, had to be disposed of because of his growing powers, his death may be termed assassination.

Thus the elimination of a king through a conspiracy, not for the purposes of gaining the throne but for the presumed welfare of a nation, is assassination. The difference, then, is one of purpose: When by his official actions and behavior, a monarch threatens to destroy the country, at least in the opinion of some special group, disposing of him may seem the only solution. An example of this type of royal assassination is the murder of PAUL I, Emperor and Czar of Russia, son and successor of Catherine the Great. He proved to be insane, and his erratic behavior, unpredictable fits of rage, and punishments of those in his disfavor caused the formation of a conspiracy to force his abdication. When he refused to give up the throne, the conspirators, crazed by fear, strangled him in 1801, the fifth year of his rule.

The reader may question whether such murders as that of the Russian Czar NICHOLAS II and his family and of RASPUTIN are assassinations. Within our definition of terms, the deaths of the royal family certainly are assassinations, because the principal reason that the killings were ordered was to rid Russia of those who were opposed to the Bolsheviks and the power structure. The symbols of absolute monarchy could not be permitted to exist. Likewise, Rasputin had to be eliminated for the good of the Czar and Czarina and their relations to the government. The Mad Monk had become too influential; the Czar often accepted the advice given by him through the Czarina who was under the monk's spell and owed an obligation to him, she thought, because of all he had done for Czarevitch Alexis.

The major assassinations which have occurred in the

United States (see Chapter 15) have been political. The murder of Negro leader Dr. Martin Luther KING, Jr., was nonpolitical, yet it may be aptly termed an assassination because his killer undoubtedly opposed civil rights for Negroes and probably, though the trial of Ray revealed neither his motives nor evidence of a conspiracy, considered King a troublemaker who was continuing to upset white power in the South. Such a powerful and influential leader should be removed "for the general good of the white people" everywhere; hence this assumed purpose makes it an assassination. On the other hand, MALCOLM X, the black nationalist leader, was murdered because his elimination was necessary to the continued success of the Black Muslim movement; the motives of the three plotters were like the power struggles between claimants to a royal throne, and his slaying was therefore murder rather than assassination as defined in this book, though the latter term was widely used. By the same evidence, the killing of George Lincoln ROCKWELL, American Nazi Party leader and rabble-rouser, in 1967, was strictly a matter of internal jealousy within the leadership, and may therefore be considered as simple murder.

Murder of underworld figures and members of rival gangs in crime syndicates such as the Mafia and Cosa Nostra, continues to be prevalent in the United States, though not as common as in the 1920's. Most of the gangland killings, called rubouts in underworld terminology, have been cold-blooded and calculated murders aimed at disposal of a rival who has encroached on a gang's territory or a gang member who has been disloyal or who is a security risk. Such individuals must be eliminated, and the means employed—machine guns, cement blocks, crushing in automobile-body flattening machines, and the like—are examples of the most barbaric types of murders, but cannot be termed assassinations.

The major element in making this often difficult distinction between the killing which is murder and that which is assassination is found in the answer to two questions. Did the slayer commit the act in the belief that he would thus rid the country or movement of a person he believed was harmful to it? Was he, in his own opinion, selfless and dedicated; that is, did he seek no personal advancement or gain, except, perhaps, the hope of becoming a martyr or hero? This distinction is sometimes difficult to pinpoint, and for that reason one must understand the background and conditions leading to the act of assassination. Particularly where conspiracies and plots are involved, the difference is often slight, since intriguers may have much to gain by the murder. An element in this distinction is that a public figure is *murdered* in his private character and assassinated in his public character.

Assassinations are committed for very complex reasons. Motives will vary; sometimes they are simple, sometimes complicated. But four types may be cited:

1) *Murders of political figures for personal reasons.* Such assassins bear a personal grievance or grudge against the victim. Sometimes, as in the case of British Prime Minister Spencer Perceval, the killer will feel that he has not been dealt with fairly or his complaint has been disregarded. The assassins of United States President James A. Garfield and

Chicago Mayor Carter Harrison were disappointed office seekers. Many other examples are included in the book.

2) *Murders by individuals suffering from mental disorder.* These are not necessarily insane persons; they may be paranoids (sufferers from delusions of persecution) or unbalanced, nervous individuals. Some of the assassins of the first type are also in this category. Charles Guiteau, who shot and killed President Garfield, may have been of this group; his trial, later discussed, was the first in the United States where insanity or mental abnormality was the contention of the defense. Leon Czolgosz, who killed President William McKinley, considered his victim the enemy of the working people. John Wilkes Booth, Lincoln's slayer, has been considered by many authorities to have been mentally disturbed. Criminologists are still puzzled by the difference between the legally sane person who is psychologically unbalanced and the insane, whether the condition is temporary or permanent.

3) *Murders as an expression of revolt against national or colonial leadership.* Such murderers are dedicated in the true sense; they pursue their ends in the honest belief that a nation will be better off with the hated individual out of the way. They are willing to accept the inevitable consequences and do not resist arrest. They admit responsibility for the crime, though they may not be willing to involve their fellow conspirators, if any. Many consider themselves martyrs and are proud of their act. Assassins in Japan and the Middle East, in fact, are applauded, praised, and even honored for their deeds by certain elements of the population.

4) *Tyrannicide.* This is defined as the act of killing a ty-

rant, who is defined as "an absolute ruler, a usurper of sovereignty, one who exercises absolute power oppressively or brutally." The Greeks and Romans praised the killing of a tyrant as the noblest human deed. In his *Republic,* Cicero wrote that the essential feature of a state is that it should be governed in accordance with law; if not so governed, he believed, it is not a state at all, but a tyranny. This is why he approved of the assassination of Julius Caesar even though he was not among the conspirators. Through the centuries there has been much justification by churchmen and philosophers for an individual taking the law into his own hands and killing a ruling tyrant rather than attempting to follow the legal process of trying a ruler for his deeds. Therefore tyrannicide has been defined as "the killing of a tyrant by a private person for the common good." One of the basic elements in the concept of tyrannicide is self-sacrifice; that is, the assassin forgets himself for the good of the state or nation.

Assassination attempts and plots have occurred in practically every country, for a prominent figure invariably, often unwittingly, incurs the enmity of citizens who feel that his death would benefit the nation. These attempted assassinations are usually the deeds of fanatics or deranged individuals. Rulers, in particular, are the victims of such bold and dedicated murderers. For example, seven attempts were made on the life of Queen Victoria, even though she was much beloved and admired by her subjects. They occurred while she was riding in her carriage in public. The assailants all used pistols and were given prison sentences or sent to mental asylums. At first such criminals in England during her reign were considered guilty of high treason, but the charge was later changed to a simple misdemeanor calling for a prison sentence or deportation. In 1872, one attempt in which live bullets were used—pistols were often unloaded or ineffective—was almost successful, and the Queen was saved only by the quick thinking of her companion, John Brown. He was rewarded with public thanks, a gold medal, and a lifetime annuity. The only injury suffered by Queen Victoria was in 1850 when she was struck violently on the head by a retired army lieutenant and suffered a black eye, severe bruises, and persistent headaches.

Every modern government leader lives more or less in constant danger. So common are plots against them that standard procedures have been introduced so that bodyguards and secret-service protection are often automatically supplied almost around the clock. Government intelligence agents and police make many unpublicized arrests. Modern heads of government accustom themselves to the necessity of such protection, and come to accept the lack of privacy and free movement which it involves. When security precautions are relaxed, the assassin is offered an unusual opportunity.

The most intensive measures being used to protect a modern head of state are those in force for the President of the United States, who is now the most securely guarded man on earth. This security system is later described in detail.

The protection given to the heads of other major nations varies according to local conditions. The British Prime Minister, for example, rides in public in an ordinary automobile with no special equipment. His official residence is guarded by several unarmed policemen. In most other nations of

Western Europe there is little outward show of protective measures; heads of state travel freely in cars with no bullet-proofing, though they are generally accompanied by policemen on motorcycles. Leaders of Communist-dominated countries are protected by inconspicuous security details.

French President Charles de Gaulle is a European exception. He was the target of at least three unsuccessful plots, and several potential assassins were arrested. The most recent attempt on his life was planned to take place on Bastille Day, July 14, 1968, when he was to review the annual parade of thousands of troops and military equipment in Paris. The plot, which was reported to West German authorities and therefore foiled, included the firing of mortars. De Gaulle made public appearances with very tight security protection. Guards were posted on the roofs of buildings near where he was to be. When he traveled, his car was flanked by crack troopers on motorbikes. Helicopters hovered overhead, and the automobile's speed was often a brisk eighty miles an hour. In towns along the route operating rooms were reserved in hospitals, and a supply of his blood type was stocked to meet a possible emergency. A team of tough judo experts accompanied him everywhere.

In the Middle East, where politics-by-assassination is almost a routine way of life, most leaders are rarely seen in public. When they do travel, heavy guards and high speeds are the rule. Black Africa's top political leaders are almost all well-guarded with large security forces. Asia's national rulers are generally provided with elaborate protection, particularly since the wave of political assassinations of the past decade. In Latin America, however, tradition demands that leaders be accessible, so nearly all Presidents are lightly guarded and often walk the streets alone without fear.

The modern assassin is continuously feared. Having formulated a plan or plot, he strikes suddenly and unexpectedly, and human and national tragedy often results.

chapter two

ASSASSINS AND THEIR PLOTS

Assassination plots may be planned by opposition groups or by an individual who nurses his personal grievances until he comes to the realization that he must take action to murder the object of his resentment in order to give vent to his feelings of outrage. A plan is always present, for assassination never occurs by accident and never on the spur of the moment. Many conspiracies are worked out over a long period, awaiting the propitious time when they may be put into action with some assurance of effectiveness. An individual is inclined to ponder long on his act, and the longer he waits, the more his antagonism toward his intended victim will be apt to increase.

The members of a group conspiring to murder generally have a common bond, familiarity with and trust of one another, and equal dedication to the final object of the plot. Quite naturally they operate secretly and become a closely knit body. The person or persons to carry out the actual killing are selected with the greatest care; they must possess the fullest confidence of their coplotters. The briefings are detailed and include alternatives, a plan of escape, and later protection of the assassin. Two types of groups are worthy of special consideration.

Nationalist groups frequently resort to violence in expressing their opposition to existing regimes. In times of turmoil they often hatch plots to assassinate political leaders, and they practice tyrannicide and regicide to get rid of their enemies. All monarchies, particularly in Europe and many of the newly developing nations, are the targets of their opposition. Throughout history, especially when boundary changes through treaties and acquisition by foreign powers have taken place, nationalist movements have been active. Following the disruption and division of the Austro-Hungarian Empire of the Hapsburg dynasty after World War I, the Balkan states were plagued with the terrorism of organized resistance.

When emerging nations are established, the vast changes involved lead to radical and vigorous opposition. The new nations of Africa are excellent contemporary examples. The struggle of India to gain freedom from Great Britain was also accompanied by tragic violence and murder.

The transition of a monarchy to a republic is almost always accompanied by well-organized opposition which frequently leads to the assassination of leaders. Die-hard monarchists and members of the displaced royal house often resist the change and resent the new leaders—the Presidents, cabinet members, and the people's representatives in the legislative bodies. The growth and development of many ex-monarchies is invariably troubled by dissident elements that use violent tactics in opposing the extensive changes in the new state.

Terrorist organizations which hatch plots to assassinate the leaders of movements which they oppose have existed to some degree in all nations, both ancient and modern. They flourish whenever new and fundamental changes in the status quo, particularly governmental reforms, are put into effect. They are formed to combat government policies of suppression; Russia under the Czars is an example. Dictators invariably encounter violent underground opposition movements, secret societies and organizations dedicated to the murder of the leader as well as his principal henchmen. Many of the Latin American leaders who have ruled despotically have been subjected to organized campaigns of terror.

The most prominent and effective of modern terrorist groups were those in Palestine before the establishment of the state of Israel. The National Military Organization (Irgun) and the Fighters for Freedom (the Stern Gang) embarked on a campaign of anti-British terrorist tactics which included assassination. Among their two most prominent victims were Lord MOYNE and Count Folke BERNADOTTE in 1948.

A comparatively new anti-Israel terrorist organization, El Fatah, composed of Arab guerrillas, now makes commando

ASSASSINS AND THEIR PLOTS

raids into Israeli territory with regularity. These activities may lead to assassination if and when the guerrillas are able to infiltrate more deeply into Israeli territory.

Whether a member of a conspiracy or acting on his own, an assassin knows definitely the reason for his act. When captured and brought to trial, he states his purpose clearly. Almost all the murders in this book include such defenses for the act. They vary widely; some are general, some personal. As Itzhak Yizernitsky, one of the three leaders of the dreaded and outlawed Stern Gang, expressed it, "A man who goes forth to kill another whom he does not know must believe one thing only—that he will change the course of history."

Regardless of the specific grievances, all assassins feel this strongly, and the political element almost always exists even though the assassin may not be aware of it.

An act of assassination always involves three elements—time, place, and weapon. The objective, the immediate death of the chosen victim, must be assured, for wounds may not prove to be fatal. Imagine the suspense of the dedicated assassin or assassins when the intended victim lingers for days, weeks, or even months under the expert care and treatment of the finest doctors, surgeons, and medical specialists and consultants who are always summoned, sometimes from long distances, to save him from death.

These three major elements in an assassination plan require the collection of much pertinent information and a detailed study of the factors involved, for there must be no loose ends that cause the attempt to fail. Since any variation in the procedure finally adopted might upset the plot, all possible contingencies must be considered. For instance, if the assassin is to strike at his victim during a parade, he must be absolutely sure that his target will be at the spot chosen at a certain time. As an example, Lee Harvey Oswald apparently planned to fire upon President John Kennedy from an upper window of the Texas School Book Depository in Dallas on November 22, 1963, just as the line of automobiles passed nearby en route to the Trade Mart, where he was to make a post-luncheon address before the Dallas Citizens' Council. As for all Presidential appearances at the time, the exact route to be followed had been printed in advance so that citizens would have the opportunity to see their President, and thousands of people lined the streets every foot of the route. Oswald knew definitely that the motorcade would be at the open area where the crowds were thinning out, to turn right and enter the Stemmons Freeway for the last lap of the ride to the Mart. Oswald needed only to complete his preparations within the Depository in advance so that he could be ready at the exact moment. Had the route been changed—the procession had slowed down while passing through the business district, even though the audience waiting at the Mart had finished their lunch, so that the crowds could be assured of seeing the Presidential party—Oswald would have been foiled in his plan.

The time chosen is therefore of major importance to intended murderers. This is particularly true in public assassinations. The many bomb plots in the Middle East were timed so that the principal victim would be killed with some of his most prominent and powerful followers.

Place is closely linked with time in an assassination plot. The locality selected will depend on whether the killer is known to his victim or has access to him through a friend or official. In most cases the assassin has seen his target from afar or has become familiar with his routines and habits. In making his preparations he will mingle anonymously with a crowd, waiting for the proper moment to make the attack.

If the assassin is known to the intended victim, the murderer will be in a position to arrange to be alone with his victim. When the killer is a part of a well-designed plot involving close associates of the target, they can always make the necessary arrangements that he be present at a designated time. If the assassin is a high-level official or a personal acquaintance, the task is even easier. Prince Youssoupov, leader of the plot to murder Rasputin, was well acquainted with his victim; their paths had crossed many times at court, and he had entertained the monk several times. When the prince invited him to his palace at midnight on December 31, 1916, Rasputin is said to have had suspicions of his intent, but accepted the invitation. The result was one of the most grotesque episodes of twentieth-century history, a blood-curdling evening of unparalleled violence before the final success of the murder.

By the very nature of their positions many public figures are readily available to their constituents. This was particularly true in the nineteenth century. The assassin of Chicago's Mayor Carter Harrison was admitted to the parlor of Harrison's home on Sunday afternoon, October 28, 1893, and the shooting was easily accomplished. At the present time, because of the climate of violence which exists throughout the world, such access is made increasingly difficult by bodyguards and secretaries who screen all visitors.

The movements of public figures are carefully watched by

would-be assassins. Their appearances at public ceremonies are almost always announced in advance, and the killer need only plan to be near enough to his victim to approach him. A shot can be fired from a great distance if the murderer is a proficient marksman, but most are aimed when the human target is near at hand. Parades where the route is lined with thousands of spectators insure the effectiveness of the act if guards around the intended victim are not too numerous.

Some of the most effective murders, however, have been executed when the mark was alone and his movements well-known. In such cases the assassin needed only to chart his course to attack at a particular moment. The assassination of Thomas D'Arcy McGee, Canadian member of Parliament, at the door of his Ottawa boarding house in 1868, is a perfect example. At a late evening session he had delivered a speech and worked in his office until the House adjourned early in the morning. McGee left the building with a fellow member. They walked together to the gateway and on for one more block (he lived but two blocks away), where his friend left him. Other members were walking nearby. McGee turned the corner of his street, on which the gaslights were not burning because of the late hour. As he arrived at his boarding house, he took out his key and put it in the latch to enter. The door was immediately pushed open from inside; simultaneously there was a sudden flash and a sharp blast of shot directly behind McGee on the street. He was killed instantly, and several people who ran to the scene found no sign of the assassin or the weapon. The killer, an ardent Fenian who resented McGee's attacks on the actions of his pro-Irish group, obviously had plotted his act with great care and knew both that the street would be dark and that McGee would return to his lodgings when the House adjourned. He had only to lie in wait to approach his intended victim.

Another perfectly carried out assassination was that of Spencer PERCEVAL, British Prime Minister and former Chancellor of the Exchequer, who was shot in the lobby of the House of Commons on May 11, 1812. John Bellingham, the murderer, had been imprisoned five years in Russia for debt. On his release and return to England he began bombarding Perceval with letters demanding redress and assistance in reestablishing his good name. The Prime Minister's failure either to grant him an interview or to take action so embittered Bellingham that he determined to avenge himself. The murder was easy to achieve; Bellingham simply waited behind a pillar in the corridor of the House, stepped forward when Perceval entered at 5:15 P.M., and fired a single pistol shot at close range. The Prime Minister staggered two or three paces, fell on his side, and then rolled on his face, dying almost instantly. Bellingham, later tried and hanged, knew that his target would be easily accessible in the corridors.

Not all assassinations take place in public, with or without crowds to conceal the assailant. A great many public figures have been killed inside, on the grounds, or at the gates of their homes—Gandhi, Trotsky, Lord Moyne, and Prime Minister Bandaranaike among others. This locale presents some advantages to the assassin or a group of murderers. The victim is more available; he does not need to be singled out in a crowd. Escape is apt to be easier, even when guards are present.

The most notable example of an intended assassin being in the right place at the right moment is probably Gavrilo Princip, the student who shot Archduke FRANZ FERDINAND and his wife SOPHIE at Sarajevo. The first attempt at bombing the car in which the royal couple was riding proved unsuccessful. By a stroke of good luck, the motorcade was halted later within ten feet of Princip because the chauffeur had not been informed of a change in route. During the short time when the driver was backing up the car to go forward on the new route, Princip fired the two shots which shook the world. He was one of several youths who had taken their places at various spots throughout the city in order to assure that the plan would succeed.

The weapon to be used is carefully selected. In the days before the invention of gunpowder and the widespread use of guns, the spear, dagger, sword, or saber were the most often used. Choking, strangulation, and suffocation were employed, particularly during the Middle Ages and in Renaissance Italy when the victim was to be personally assaulted at close hand. Poison has seldom been used except in murders. The very nature of assassination assumes the use of a weapon in the hands of the killer.

Guns of all types have been used by most modern assassins. Depending on the distance between the killer and his victim, the types include the pistol and revolver for close attack and the rifle, of various bores, for longer distances, when the user is in concealment. Since World War I, machine guns of all types have been widely used, particularly to kill a target when in a crowd or an automobile.

Allied with guns was the bomb. Its use was greatest during the activities of the anarchists in the second half of the nineteenth century, and it has often been used in more recent times when a group is to be attacked and the murderer or murderers hope to kill a prime target who will be present.

Most assassinations come as a surprise to the victim, even when threats have been made and conspiracies well-known or rumored. The victim is usually caught off guard; he looks into the muzzle of a gun or is shot and dead before the assassin can be stopped. This element of surprise is foremost in all assassination plots; the killer has outlined his plan so carefully and in such detail that the final thrust is sudden and well aimed and, in most cases, results in immediate death. Only when unforeseen developments alter the plans do wounds result instead of the instant death which is the objective of the assailant or assailants.

Actual confrontations, other than a momentary recognition of his attacker by the target, are rare. Before dying, Caesar reproached his friend Brutus in the famous phrase *"Et tu, Brute."* The lengthy conversation of Thomas à Becket with his killers is almost unprecedented; not only did the archbishop remind them of the implications of their proposed act, but he denounced them.

When an assassination attempt is unsuccessful, the results may often prove disastrous. The protection of the target will be substantially increased, and if the conspirators are discovered, the punishments meted out may be sufficient to discourage any further attempts. In addition, the leader who has escaped death may wreak his vengeance in an outpouring of violence and oppression.

The 1944 plot against Hitler by his disenchanted generals is an excellent example. A handful of army officers had made a number of attempts to kill their supreme commander during 1943. In March they had almost succeeded; the commanding general of the Russian front had planted a time bomb in the plane in which the Führer was to return to Germany. But the mechanism failed, the bomb did not explode, and a revolt in Berlin timed to begin on receipt of the announcement of Hitler's death in a "plane accident" had to be hastily canceled. By midsummer of 1944 the Nazi fortunes were declining. The Anglo-American forces under General Eisenhower had landed in Normandy, and the handwriting on the wall indicated that the Reich was doomed.

On July 22, 1944, Colonel Klaus von Stauffenberg left Berlin to report on the military situation at a high-level conference with Hitler, who was at the East Prussian front. In his briefcase the colonel carried a bomb similar to the one used unsuccessfully the previous year; it had no clock mechanism whose ticking might lead to its discovery. The key to the possible success was a thin wire which was in a capsule containing a corrosive acid. When the colonel broke the capsule, the wire would dissolve in ten minutes, and the bomb would then explode.

Stauffenberg broke the capsule just before he entered the room where the military conference with two dozen high command officers was in progress. He seated himself a few feet to one side of Hitler and placed the briefcase under the table about six feet from the Führer's legs. As the conversations continued, with less than ten minutes remaining before the bomb would detonate, the colonel told the officer next to him that he must make a telephone call, and left the council room. The briefcase blocked this officer's feet, and he moved it to the far side of the heavy table support, away from Hitler.

Just as the Führer asked one of the generals to summon Stauffenberg to give his report, the bomb went off. The time was 12:42 P.M. The conference hall was destroyed in a roar of smoke and flame. One of the officers had been killed and several severely wounded. Though badly shaken, Hitler was not seriously wounded. By the time the colonel had arrived in Berlin to direct the revolt there as planned, the news that the Führer was alive rendered any actions useless. Stauffenberg was shot by a firing squad before midnight.

The resulting vengeance was horrible, with thousands of suspects imprisoned and many executed. Several officers involved committed suicide. Hitler subsequently became even more cruel, and relentlessly pushed his generals until the final collapse of the Third Reich.

Many unsuccessful attempts are discussed in subsequent chapters. These failures always resulted in a tightening of security to prevent further assaults.

When assassination plots are successful, swift reprisals may follow. Punishment will include the guilty, the suspected, and, in all too many cases, the innocent. Punitive measures are most likely to occur in police states and dictatorships where suspicion is rife. A notorious example took place after the 1942 assassination of Reinhard HEYDRICH, Nazi chief of Security Police and governor of Bohemia and Moravia.

The successful murder was carried out on the morning of May 29 by two Czech patriots of the Czechoslovak Army in England who had been parachuted near Prague from a

Royal Air Force airplane. While Heydrich was driving in his open Mercedes from his country villa to his headquarters, a bomb of British make was tossed at him, blowing the car to pieces and shattering his spine. The two assailants made their escape under a smoke screen and were given refuge by priests of a Prague church. To revenge this outrage the Nazi occupation government executed 1,331 Czechs, including 201 women. The actual assassins, along with 120 members of the Czech resistance, were besieged in the church by the S.S., the Nazi special police force, and all were killed. The Gestapo never learned that the two assassins were among the dead. The final and most outrageous act of reprisal was the razing of the village of Lidice on June 10. All the men and boys over sixteen were shot, and the women and children sent to concentration camps. Lidice was wiped off the face of the earth and today is a monument to Nazi ferocity and cruelty.

Assassins have been the subject of many studies by psychologists. In these studies, the lone assassin has been revealed as a victim of paranoid schizophrenia—that is, he has delusions of persecution and is removed from reality. All assassins share the belief that they are totally right and that their act is justified, because in their minds they are eliminating a great evil.

Many of the murders recounted in this book include this objective as stated by the assassins under police questioning or in trials. Dr. John Spiegel, who directs Brandeis University's Lemberg Center for the Study of Violence, in speaking of the assassinations of the four United States Presidents, has stated, "There is a direct link between assassins and social conflict. Every assassin's self-assessment of himself is that he is performing his act in a just cause. And that cause is usually political." The killer is proud of what criminal psychiatrist Frederic Wertham calls "magnicide—the killing of somebody prominent." Even the slightly mentally deranged share this presumption, and often sincerely believe that God or a superior power ordered them to kill. A few examples of this feeling will indicate the intensity of the conviction.

The boy who assassinated the Earl of Mayo, when asked at his trial why he performed the act, replied, "By the order of God." When the prosecutor questioned him about his associates, he said "Among men I have no accomplice; God is my partner."

In a tribute to Abbas Aqa for his murder of Persian Premier Amin-es-Sultan in 1907, a Teheran newspaper stated:

> Yea, every one who lays down his dear life for the Salvation of his people and his country's cause, and spends the coin of his existence for the ransom of the nation and the constitution, ought to be respected by his Countrymen with a respect exceeding that due to their own spirits and bodies, and to be an evident proof of God's mercy.
>
> In truth, as a consequence of the blow struck by this brave youth, such a change has been wrought in the course of affairs in this kingdom as could not have been accomplished by several millions of money or fifty thousand soldiers. . . . All is safe and tranquil, all the nobles and barons have sworn the most solemn oaths of fidelity; the National Assembly enjoys internal order, the Deputies are disciplined, the power of the disloyal is broken.

This dedication of Middle East assassins, a holdover from the days of the Hashasheen, still prevails. For example, newspapers reported that Sirhan Sirhan, the Jordanian immigrant who shot Senator Robert Kennedy, was "shocked and reacted emotionally" when the lawyer for his defense asked a prospective juror how she would vote if "willful, deliberate, premeditated" murder was proved. When she answered that the penalty would be death, the prosecutor remarked that most of the jurors already selected considered it was a political assassination. Later Sirhan asked his lawyer to make sure that he had heard the words "political assassination" correctly, and the attorney explained to him, "In this country political assassination is different from murder." The lawyer then told reporters, "We get dozens of letters from people abroad, sending us money and telling us that Sirhan should not be treated as an ordinary murderer, that 'he killed for his country'."

It is important to realize that the target of an assassination is rarely the individual himself; it is what he stands for. The act is not personal. For example, David Pratt, after his unsuccessful attempt on the life of the South African Prime Minister, said, "I think I was shooting at all apartheid rather than at Dr. Verwoerd."

Another common characteristic of assassins is that they are usually obscure, often very ordinary men. In their minds the act gives them a self-importance which is nonexistent in their lives. This, combined with the idea of dedication to a cause, creates their moment of glory, whether the consequences are imprisonment or death. In the long trials they become the center of attention. For the first time, perhaps, they are listened to attentively and patiently, and they are able to put into words their convictions and emotions. Since the possibility, almost assurance, of death has been accepted by them, they need not be timid for fear of their lives.

The background of most modern assassins shows a history of failure and frustration. They have been unable to obtain work, and if they have, their performance has been either poor or a failure. Almost without exception they have been loners detached or separated from their families or lacking family ties of any permanence.

These are the murderers who are enemies of society who with dagger thrust, gunshot, and bomb throwing cause national and worldwide shock, sorrow, and political upheaval.

chapter three

TWO BIBLICAL ASSASSINATIONS

Following the enslavement of the Hebrews in Egypt and the exodus under Moses, Canaan (Palestine) was conquered by Joshua. There followed what is called the period of the "judges" of Israel, from about 1300 to 1030 B.C. These judges were people who were, in practical terms, rulers of the people before the establishment of the monarchy, the united kingdom under Saul, David, and Solomon in about 1030 to 822 B.C.

Judges, the seventh book of the Bible, recounts the activities of the tribes, warning against the beleaguered Israelites led by a series of judges who were their champions and heroes, delivering them from their enemies in a series of wars in all parts of Palestine. The successes of the various tribes were generally followed by periods of peace ranging from eighteen to forty years. Their unconquerable spirit and dedication carried them through this struggle for existence. Two gruesome assassinations, among the first recorded in ancient times, took place during this period—the murder of Eglon, King of Moab, by Ehud the Benjamite, and of Sisera, a Canaanite general, by Jael, the wife of Heber the Kenite.

THE FAT KING AND THE LEFT-HANDED KILLER
King Eglon (early twelfth century B.C.)

Ehud, of the tribe of Benjamin and the great-grandson of Benjamin, was the second of the series of judges. The Moabites, together with the Amalekites and Ammonites, had taken Jericho from the Israelites and held them captive for eighteen years. Ehud was left-handed, a condition not at all rare at the time since the tribe of Benjamin was said to have had seven hundred left-handed men who had become so skillful in the use of the left hand that they "could sling stones and never miss their targets." Their conqueror, King EGLON, was called "the Fat" because he weighed almost three hundred pounds, "a very fat man," according to the biblical account. "Eglon" means "young bull." (*Interpretive Bible,* Vol. 2, p. 38.) His rule was tyrannical, and the Benjamites waited eighteen years until their leader Ehud received a divine commission from God, or Yahveh, to destroy the oppressor. Ehud is called "a deliverer" in Judges

3:15. The story of the assassination is told in detail in Judges 3:16–23.

When King Eglon imposed an outrageous tax upon his captives, Ehud took action. A tribute was to be paid to the monarch, and Ehud decided to use this occasion to murder the enemy of his tribe. To prepare himself, he made a double-edged dagger, fashioned to order for a fat man. It was a cubit—about eighteen inches—in length. Since Ehud was left-handed, he strapped the weapon to his right thigh ("did gird it under his raiment upon his right thigh"), where he could more readily draw it and where it would be less likely to draw attention.

After the tribute had been delivered to the King, Ehud dismissed the bearers and, claiming to have a personal message from Yahveh, was granted a private audience. Eglon was sitting alone in a "summer parlor" when Ehud entered the room, and as the King rose to greet his visitor, Ehud "put forth his left hand and took the dagger from his right thigh, and thrust it into his belly. And the haft also went in after the blade; and the fat closed upon the blade, so that he could not draw the dagger out of his belly; and the dirt came out." (Judges 3:21–22)

After his bloody deed was accomplished, Ehud locked the doors of the room in which his victim lay and made his escape. The narrative describes the increasing anxiety of King Eglon's servants when the chamber remained silent. Finally, we are told, "they took a key and opened [the doors]; and behold, their lord was fallen down dead on the earth."

Ehud immediately rallied the Israelites who were encamped in the mountain fortresses of Ephraim. He blew a trumpet "and the children of Israel went down with him from the mount, and he before them. And he said unto them, Follow after me: for the Lord hath delivered your enemies the Moabites into your hand." They quickly seized the fords over the Jordan River and blocked the escape of the trapped Moabites. "And they slew of Moab at that time about ten thousand men, all lusty, and all men of valour: and there escaped not a man.

"So Moab was subdued that day under the hand of Israel: and the land had rest fourscore years."

Ehud was considered a great judge, and for his act was regarded as a God-inspired deliverer.

A WIFE MURDERS HER HUSBAND'S FRIEND
Sisera (1150 B.C.)

Living among the Canaanites, the ten tribes, without a central government, worshiped Jehovah and regarded themselves as a part of Israel, though in bondage.

At this time, a woman judge became their leader. Allying herself with Barak, the military leader of Israel, Deborah, to whom Joan of Arc has been compared, inspired and united them to battle against their Canaanite enemy SISERA, who had assembled a force of nine hundred chariots and armed them with iron weapons to meet the weak and light-armed foe. Deborah (Judges 4:9) proclaimed that the ten thousand Israelites were to be guided by the Lord, and prophesied that "the Lord shall sell Sisera into the hand of a woman."

Aroused by Deborah, the Hebrews left the safety of the mountains and advanced on Sisera's forces waiting below on the plain of Esdraelon. The Lord was indeed on their side, for a devastating storm broke and as the water rolled down the mountains, it created a flash flood in the Kishon River on the plain. When the river overflowed its banks, the heavy chariots of Sisera became mired in the mud and the Israelites drove the panic-stricken Canaanites into the river and "all the host of Sisera fell upon the edge of the sword, and there was not a man left" (Judges 4:14–16). King Sisera fled from his defeated forces and sought refuge in the tent of a friend, Heber the Kenite. However, only his wife Jael was there. Ignoring her protests, her husband had betrayed to Sisera the location of the Israelite forces, and he was therefore sure that he would find protection and safety.

The Kenites were a nomadic tribe living in tents made of cloth woven from goat's hair. Wherever they settled, the women set up the tents, stretching the cloth by long ropes fastened into the ground by wooden pegs. The pegs were driven into the ground with a wooden hammer or mallet.

When Sisera sought refuge, Jael welcomed her husband's friend with a smile. The story is told in Judges 4:17–22. "Turn in, my lord, turn in to me; fear not," she called to Sisera. Sure that he had found a safe hiding place among friendly people, he went into the tent.

"Give me a little water to drink," he panted, for he was near exhaustion. Jael gave him a drink from a skin of goat's milk, and when he lay down upon a sleeping pallet, she covered him up with a mantle. "Stand in the door of the tent," Sisera directed her. "If any man comes and asks if there is a man here, say no."

Jael pretended to do as he had asked, but a plan had formed in her mind. As soon as he was asleep, she took a tent pin and a mallet, and holding the pin in one hand and the hammer in the other, drove the pin home with firm strokes through the skull of Sisera and into the ground. Once or twice his body jerked convulsively and then was still.

Barak and his men, in pursuit of Sisera, would have passed the tent of Heber, but Jael went out to meet them. "I will shew thee the man whom thou seekest." she said proudly. And when he came into her tent, "Sisera lay dead, and the nail was in his temples" (Judges 4:22).

That night, at a great feast of celebration, Deborah composed a song of praise to the Lord (Judges 5) which paid tribute to Jael's exploit:

> Blessed above women shall Jael the wife of Heber the Kenite be, blessed shall she be above women in the tent. He asked water and she gave him milk; she brought forth butter in a lordly dish. She put her hand to the nail, and her right hand to the workmen's hammer; and with the hammer she smote Sisera, she smote off his head, when she had pierced and stricken through his temples. At her feet he bowed, he fell, he lay down: at her feet he bowed, he fell; where he bowed, there he fell down dead.
>
> The mother of Sisera looked out at a window, and cried through the lattice, Why is his chariot so long in coming? why tarry the wheels of his chariots? . . . Have they not sped? Have they not divided the prey? . . .
>
> So let all thine enemies perish, O Lord: but let them that love him be as the sun when he goeth forth in his might.

The victorious Israelites conquered Sisera's successor, "and the land had rest forty years."

The Old Testament is filled with stories of other murders and assassinations, for the road to final unity and full possession of their homeland under the various kingdoms was a long one.

chapter four

DAGGERS AND SWORDS IN ANCIENT ROME

THE IDES OF MARCH
Julius Caesar (March 15, 44 B.C.)

The Roman statesman and general, Gaius Julius CAESAR, as one of his numerous biographers has put it, "excelled in war, in politics, in statesmanship, in letters, in oratory, and in social grace." The story of his achievements is a long one —as a friend of the people, organizer of the First Triumvirate with Pompey and Crassus, as consul, as leader in the Gallic wars, as civil-war leader, and as pursuer of his sworn enemy, Pompey, to Egypt where he formed his notorious liaison with Cleopatra. He returned triumphantly to Rome in 47 B.C. becoming tribune of the people for life and dictator. He was indeed master of Rome. The events from that time on led to his assassination in 44 B.C.

As a dictator he acted always to consolidate his own position and to reduce the formerly powerful Senate to a secondary position. His powers were absolute, and he became a tyrant. Honors continued to be heaped upon him; for example, the month of Quintillis in which he was born was renamed Julius (July), and he was deified as a major god. He was offered the title of king, but refused it.

When the conspiracy against him was first hatched is not known. Cassius was the ringleader, and he persuaded Marcus Brutus to join, though Brutus and Caesar were the best of friends. There were more than sixty conspirators, and many had been Caesar's trusted and close friends. The avowed object of the plot was tyrannicide, the killing of a tyrant, which in the eyes of both Greeks and Romans was righteous and just. A dictatorship of one-man rule was harmful to the Republic, and if it continued they would derive no financial gains and their political power would vanish. The Senate was already a governing body in name only, its powers limited by Caesar's whims and ambitions. All would change once he was removed.

They decided to strike on March 15 (the Ides of March), when the Senate was to meet in the theater of Pompey. That morning Caesar's wife Calpurnia begged him to cancel the meeting, because in a dream she had seen him streaming with blood. But he was not one to believe in dreams and soothsayers. Since the members of the Senate were sworn to protect him, he believed he had nothing to fear.

When he did not arrive at the appointed hour, the conspirators sent Brutus, his devoted friend, to bring him. He was of course completely unarmed, draped in the toga which Roman citizens wore on ceremonial occasions. The conspirators also wore togas under which they concealed daggers.

As Caesar entered and seated himself on his gilded chair, one of the conspirators came up to present a petition. Other senators crowded around as though to back his request. Suddenly, Casca, directly behind Caesar, drew his dagger for the first stroke. Caesar wrapped his toga around his left arm and struck back with his stylus, the long iron pencil the Romans used for writing on wax tablets. A second senator seized hold of his purple toga and pulled it away to expose his neck. Caesar rose from his chair and threw him to the ground. The other assassins then closed in on him. Cassius wounded him in the face, and when Brutus struck him in the thigh, Caesar cried out, "You too, Brutus?" before falling down dead. Those senators not involved in the plot remained frozen in terror. Caesar had received twenty-three wounds.

Once Caesar was killed, the conspirators had intended to speak in the Senate, but in panic the senators had fled, and instead the plotters ran out to the Forum, crying, "Liberty! Liberty!"

The Senate appointed Antony, the surviving consul, to succeed Caesar. Though bound to punish the conspirators, the senators realized that if Caesar were condemned as a tyrant, all his acts would become illegal, and they were afraid of the people's reaction. Instead they accepted Cicero's suggestion that a general amnesty be declared and that no inquiry should be made.

At the public funeral, Caesar's will was read first, followed by many tributes. Antony gave the customary oration, which has been immortalized in Shakespeare's play. When Caesar's body was cremated, the assembled mob went wild with fury. They set fire to the Senate chamber where he had been murdered, then dispersed to burn the homes of the conspirators, who had fled.

Eighteen-year-old Octavius, Caesar's grand-nephew and protégé, had been adopted as his chief heir under the name Julius Caesar Octavianus. He returned to Rome as Octavian. There, opposed by Cicero and the powerful Mark Antony, Octavian embarked on thirteen remorseless years of murder and civil war, until at thirty-two he emerged as Augustus Caesar, sole master of the Roman world.

A CRITIC MEETS DEATH
Marcus Tullius Cicero (December 7, 43 B.C.)

The greatest Roman orator—perhaps the greatest orator of any age or any country—CICERO was also Rome's greatest prose writer. But he was more than a speaker and writer; he was also a politician and a philosopher, and his influence in the Republic was great.

Cicero's most influential political writing was *De Republica (The Republic)*, in which he outlined the purpose and structure of this ideal against the rule of a dictator. Political scientists still consider this an important work, for centuries later Cicero's ideas were still valid and applicable.

The entry of Cicero into the Roman political scene began in 63 B.C. when he became a consul, or magistrate, after a law career during which his reputation as an orator became established. He was always thereafter a leader in the Senate and used his influence in this position continuously and to good effect.

His relations with Julius Caesar before and during the dictatorship varied. Being outspoken, he sometimes supported, sometimes opposed, Caesar. Though not involved in the assassination plot, he approved of it because the centralization of power in one man was against all his principles. It was he who proposed the general amnesty which followed the assassination.

Cicero and Mark Antony bitterly hated one another. When Octavian returned to Rome, he attempted to preserve the Republic as it had been. When he broke with the Senate, Octavian realized that the Republic was dead and that all hopes for its revival were doomed. As was usual when new governments were set up, a list of the enemies of the state, called proscription, was compiled. The arrest and execution of the prominent men thus named and the confiscation of their property followed. In a series of orations called the Philippics, Cicero had attacked Antony devastatingly, restating his ideal of the Republic. When the Second Triumvirate was established, Antony demanded the heads of the men who had openly attacked him in the Senate. This was the death warrant for Cicero; his name headed the proscription list, which included three hundred senators and two thousand citizens. Whoever could do so, fled from Rome.

Cicero was tempted to accompany his wife, but realized

the inevitability of his death. He decided to wait quietly, but friends managed to convince him that it was foolhardy of him to remain, and he set out in a litter to the port of embarkation.

He was pursued by a band of Antony's soldiers led by a centurion who bore a personal grudge against him. When the group overtook him, Cicero forbade his slaves and attendants to defend him, and leaned forward in his litter. The centurion immediately beheaded him by a single stroke of his sword. His hands were cut off and sent to Rome for public display over the rostrum of the Senate as a horrible example. Antony's wife cut off Cicero's tongue which so often had railed against her husband.

So ended the life and career of an opponent of the government who fearlessly spoke out against all he considered evil.

chapter five

∧∧∧∧∧∧∧∧∧∧∧∧∧∧∧∧∧∧∧∧∧∧∧∧∧∧∧∧∧∧∧

MURDER IN A CATHEDRAL

Thomas a Becket, Archbishop of Canterbury (December 29, 1170)

One of the most famous assassinations in history is without doubt the murder of the highest religious figure in medieval England. His death in Canterbury cathedral is a model example of assassination in contrast to murder in that his slayers—whether or not with King Henry II's complicity—sincerely felt that he should be disposed of for the benefit of the monarchy: He was an enemy of the state and he opposed many of its policies; he was therefore a dangerous man. Had he been murdered so that his attackers might occupy his post, the act might be considered as simple murder. Because of the motives involved, however, the slaying exhibits well the sometimes tenuous distinction between murder and political assassination.

The dispute between the archbishop and the monarch formed one of the most notable struggles between church and state in all history. The solution by assassination was almost unparalleled; it was shocking and offensive to the people, and King Henry was to undergo unusual criticism and personal torment and regret as a result.

Henry II, who ascended the English throne in 1154, centralized the government in the royal authority and strengthened the royal courts. His concept of his kingly prerogatives was that the Church should be included, that the church-state relationship should be governed by the royal authority. This issue was not to be settled until almost four centuries later during the reign of Henry VIII.

THOMAS À BECKET was of Norman birth. When he was thirty-five, he was taken into the household of Theobald, archbishop of Canterbury, and was a deacon when Henry came to the throne. He gained the attention of the young King and became an intimate friend and adviser. As the royal chancellor, he was what might be called the King's secretary, and his power was next to that of the monarch.

Though he had notable success in uniting the elements of his kingdom, Henry was unable to prevail against the power of the English Church. When Theobald died in 1161, the King persuaded Thomas to become the archbishop of Canterbury. With some misgiving, because he realized that he would be involved in a struggle with his master, Thomas accepted the appointment, though he was not even ordained a priest until the day before his consecration as head of the English Church.

In making the appointment, however, the King made a grave miscalculation, for Thomas had no sooner accepted it than he completely changed. He gave up his previous lavish and materialistic way of living and became a devout and sincere churchman. Thomas, in short, refused to serve two masters. The disagreements between the two multiplied so rapidly, with the archbishop staunch in his loyalty to the Church, that in 1164 Thomas went into self-exile in France for six years. He returned in December, 1170, only when Henry humbled himself by making generous concessions and promises based on their former friendship.

Their relationship deteriorated rapidly. Thomas proved unbending in opposing Henry's continued attempt to seize the power of the Church. A showdown was inevitable, for the feeling between them ran high. The breaking point was reached when Thomas, with the approval of the Pope himself, suspended the bishops who had taken part in the coronation of Henry's son by the archbishop of York in direct violation of both precedent and constitutional law. On Christmas day, 1170, from the pulpit of his own cathedral, he pronounced the excommunication of all who had assisted at the prince's coronation. Four days later he was dead.

On midafternoon of December 29, four barons from France, where Henry was on a visit, arrived at the archbishop's palace and demanded an interview with Thomas as royal officers sent on an official mission. In a long session, they presented the King's demands—that Thomas recognize and pay honor to the young king, absolve the bishops, and be tried in the royal court. Thomas stood firm and based his refusal on the power "given me by God and my lord the Pope." The laws of the Church had been violated, he said, and these were above the temporal power of the monarchy. After they had left, Thomas realized that he had sealed his doom but told his intimates that he was prepared to die.

After the four knights had donned their armor, they went with some followers to the archbishop's bedroom, where he was locked in with his advisers, and attempted to batter down the door without success. At five o'clock Thomas entered the cathedral in a procession headed by a cross bearer. When he reached the interior of the church through the cloisters, he commanded that the doors be unlocked. "Christ Church is not a fortress," he said. He and his retainers obviously believed that no men, even emissaries from the King himself, would have the temerity to violate the sanctuary. Almost immediately the four knights burst into the cathedral, demanding to meet the archbishop face to face.

The murder of the archbishop did not take place in the sanctuary, for Becket moved toward his would-be killers and actually confronted them. This was no swift, sudden, and surprising murder; not only did he identify the members of the murder party, but he spoke to them. Nor was this killing a private affair, for scores of witnesses—monks, choir members, citizens, clerks, and servants of the archbishop's household—frozen by the audacity and outright horror of the act became rooted in their places and could only silently witness the act. Others fled in panic; some of his closest followers, fearing for their own safety, quit the spot in terror. Their immediate reaction was that the King's men might expand the attack to include anyone who was a loyal follower of Becket. But this was one murder in which observers both heard the preliminaries and witnessed the fearful act itself.

The assassination was not a usual one. To the twelfth-century Englishman, the Church was the state; separation was to come many years later. The archbishop, though a politician and statesman, was in truth the highest spiritual leader of the people. Even to plot his death was outrageous and daring. To carry out the act was indeed treason.

Thus on this fateful night the stage had been set for the encounter. It came as no surprise to Thomas that his feud with his King and master would come to a head. The denouement was inevitable.

"Where is the archbishop?" cried the leader, Reginald Fitzurse. Thomas answered immediately from the darkness of the choir, "A priest as well as archbishop. If you seek me, you will find me here," and he moved to them. Three of the knights surrounded him, and one demanded, "Absolve the bishops you have excommunicated."

"I have already said what I will and will not do," Thomas answered.

"If you do not, you are a dead man," answered one of the four.

"I am ready to die for God and the Church," said Thomas. His refusal to surrender was final.

The knights seized him with the intention of carrying him out of the church, but Thomas resisted, struck them, and threw Fitzurse to the floor. The knight whirled his sword in a circle over the archbishop's head, barely grazing it. Thomas attempted no further resistance. "I commend myself and my Church to God," he said in almost a whisper.

One of the knights sprang forward and brought his sword down toward Thomas' head. The only one of the archbishop's attendants who had remained threw up his arms to intercept the blow; the blade cut deep into his arm, was only partly deflected, and sliced into the crown on Thomas' head with such force that blood gushed over his eyes and face.

"Strike, strike!" a knight called to the others as he raised his sword again and once more brought it down on the bleeding head. Thomas could still speak and he stood unmoving. "Into thy hands, O Lord, I commend my spirit," he said. At a third blow he fell to his hands and knees as he murmured, "For the name of Jesus and the defense of the Church, I embrace death." As he lay there, one of the knights gave him the death blow, striking with such tremendous force that he cut off the top of Thomas' head and shattered his blade in two on the pavement. "The blood whitened with brain and the brain reddened with blood, dyeing the floor of the cathedral," a witness wrote later. To complete the horror, one of the assassins' followers placed his foot on the dead man's neck, inserted his sword into the enormous open wound, and scattered brains and blood over the pavement. "Let us go, knights," he then said. "This fellow will not rise again."

The ghastly and brutal murder shocked the whole of the Christian world, and the tomb of Thomas in Canterbury became a shrine. He was canonized in 1173. Though it has been generally agreed that the King was not directly responsible for Thomas' death, there can be no doubt that he was indirectly responsible.

Public opinion and his own realization of the enormity of the act caused the King four years later to make public penance at the scene of the murder and to pay for an expedition to the Holy Land. Thomas continued to be regarded as a martyr, and his tomb was the focus of holy pilgrimages. In 1538 when the final separation of Church and State was achieved by Henry VIII, this physical reminder of the churchman who even in death had opposed the crown was destroyed.

chapter six

A CRUSADER-VICTIM OF THE HASHASHEEN

Conrad of Montferrat (1192)

The series of wars undertaken by the European Christians to recover the Holy Land from Islam (the Muslims) is a unique event in history. The motives for these nine long journeys, which took place between 1095 and 1272, were comparatively simple.

Jerusalem was taken by the Muslim Caliph Omar in the seventh century. At first Christians were permitted to make pilgrimages to the Holy Sepulcher, but soon they began to

A CRUSADER-VICTIM OF THE HASHASHEEN

be persecuted and the Church defiled. In 1095 Pope Urban II urged Christendom to war, promising that the journey would count as full penance for any sins. Crusading at first for religious motives, the nobles later began to seek loot and the acquisition of cities and lands. These latter motives led them to become the sworn enemies of the Hashasheen, the Ismaili sect that gave our vocabulary the term "assassin." From mountain fortresses in Persia, Iraq, and Syria, the Hashasheen first attacked their enemies, particularly followers of the Caliph of Baghdad. Scores of leaders in the Middle East, including Egypt, became victims of these dedicated murderers. Eventually any lord, infidel or Christian, was blackmailed for tribute, land, and castles, always with the threat of murder. The Crusaders came in contact with the Syrian Hashasheen branch, beginning in the third crusade (1189–92) led by Emperor Frederick I of Germany, Philip II of France, and Richard I (the Lion-Hearted) of England, following the capture of Jerusalem by Saladin, the Muslim warrior and sultan of Egypt.

Though previous Crusaders had bargained with the assassins, their first and most important victim was CONRAD, Marquis of Montferrat, a region of northern Italy, who had set out from Constantinople for the Holy Land with a company of French Crusaders in 1187. When he reached the port of Acre in Palestine, he learned that the army of Jerusalem had been destroyed and had yielded to Saladin. Saladin was holding his father captive there, so Conrad sailed on to Tyre, which was occupied by infidels, the general term for any non-Christian. Conrad seized the city and held it as an almost impregnable stronghold, and Tyre became the headquarters of the Crusaders who still harbored the hope of defeating Saladin and winning the Holy Land a second time. Saladin, hated by the Hashasheen, had already been their target twice, while he was besieging Aleppo. Hired by the ruler of the city in return for lands and money, a band penetrated his camp in 1174 but were recognized. The next year, disguised as soldiers in his army, they attacked him with knives, but his armor saved him.

Meanwhile, Conrad became King of Jerusalem by marrying Isabella, the daughter of Amalric, the Latin King of the city. He attempted to patch up his differences with Guy of Lusignan, the former Frankish King who had abdicated, in order to consolidate the Crusaders into a strong force. Disagreements and enmities between the various leaders characterized the Third Crusade, leading to a power struggle. The lofty aims of the Crusaders became of secondary importance when the King of France and the King of England arrived. The leader, the German Emperor, drowned in Asia Minor while en route south, and the Crusade fell apart. Enemies of Conrad joined with Richard I just as the siege of Acre was stalemated. Richard and Philip captured the stronghold, and Richard set about to conciliate the differences between Guy and Conrad.

Conrad was never crowned. Riding home from a banquet, he was attacked by two young Hashasheen disguised as monks and stabbed to death. One of them struck him with a knife, the other fled into a church nearby. The wounded marquis was carried into the same church by his friends. When the companion of the assassin saw that Conrad was still alive, he rushed toward him and struck him again. This dagger thrust was fatal.

These two Hashasheen, seized and tortured and crucified by the Franks, confessed that Richard had hired them. Histories have devoted many pages to the charge that the English King instigated the murder, but the accusation has been proved false. He was never near the strongholds of the Assassins and never had any dealings with them. The two assassins were undoubtedly hired by others eager to be rid of Conrad.

The death of Conrad, the one man Saladin feared, healed the long feud that had divided the Crusaders. Philip returned to France, and Richard made a truce with Saladin before returning to England. In this aspect, the Third Crusade was a success, but the struggle for the Holy Land and Jerusalem continued for almost a century.

chapter seven

A LEADER OF THE FRENCH REVOLUTION

Jean-Paul Marat (July 13, 1793)

The overthrow of the long-established French monarchy, with its two-class social system was accomplished between the years 1792 and 1799, seven bloody years almost unmatched in history. The great struggle for government by and for the people was characterized by surging mobs shouting the *"Marseillaise,"* the crashing blade of the guillotine, heads rolling into bloody baskets, power struggles among monarchists, republicans, and liberals, and above all by leaders who were giants of good and evil.

One of the leaders was Jean-Paul MARAT, "the friend of the people," full of ideals and words, and thirsty for blood. Before the time of the Revolution he had established a successful career as a respected and expert doctor. When it began, he abandoned medicine for politics, founding a journal, *L'Ami du Peuple* (*The Friend of the People*), in which he expressed his hatred and suspicion of all who were in power. When outlawed, he published his paper from various hiding places, mainly the cellars of friends, ruthlessly attacking the personalities of the day and inciting the people to violence. While hiding in the sewers of Paris, he contracted a skin disease which covered his unattractive face with ugly splotches and caused migraine headaches. His inflammatory articles indirectly caused the September massacres in 1792, in which thousands of arrests were made and over a thousand "enemies of the state" executed.

Shortly after, he was able to return to public life when he was elected to the National Convention as a radical Jacobin. The number of deputies was 750. One hundred were Jacobins, the party of the bourgeoisie, and 165 were Girondists, who were opposed to mob action. The remainder, the majority of the deputies, were uncommitted. Marat stepped up attacks in his journal and was able to increase his power. The struggle between the Jacobins and the Girondists centered on what to do with the royal family. Louis XVI appeared before the Convention, was tried, and beheaded in January, 1793. This lost battle caused the downfall of the Girondists and marked the triumph of Marat. He began to collect the names of the Girondists who were fomenting an attack on him. His assassin was able to meet and kill him because she pretended to have knowledge of Girondist activities in Normandy.

While Marat was playing out his role as a friend of the people, a twenty-five-year-old girl named Marianne Charlotte de Corday d'Armont (shortened to Charlotte Corday) was living quietly in Caen, Normandy. As a young girl she had been an avid reader, particularly of Corneille, a distant relative of her family. Her favorite reading was Plutarch's *Lives;* her favorite heroine Judith, murderess, in the Apocrypha, of the general Holofernes; and her favorite hero Brutus, who murdered Julius Caesar. At her trial she admitted that she considered the latter two models leading to her act. Charlotte had spent several years in a nunnery and had expected to take the veil, but when the Revolution closed all convents, she had returned to the home of an aunt.

Caen had become a refuge for Girondist deputies who had been expelled from the Convention. Being of a romantic and emotional turn of mind, Charlotte conceived a hatred of all Jacobins who had caused their misery, particularly Marat, whom she regarded as responsible for all the country's difficulties. The more she heard of them through those who had been his victims, the more she became convinced that he was a monster and that posterity would praise the man or woman who put an end to his life. She would become a martyr by performing the act, and so she determined to go to Paris and kill him.

The pretext she needed to meet him face to face was easily found. Her contact with the local refugees had been made by seeking their aid and advice on behalf of a friend of her convent days whose property had been seized and pension canceled when the convents throughout France were closed. They advised her that the sponsorship and recommendation of any person then in power would be valuable in her attempts on her friend's behalf. Immediately Marat came to mind; he was at the zenith of his power, and this would be her excuse for visiting him in Paris.

She prepared for the murder with care and deliberation. She told her friends that she was going to Argentan to see her father, but wrote him instead that she was going to England because of the turmoil in France.

When she reached Paris, Charlotte learned that Marat was ill. He was both exhausted and suffering from a recurrent attack of the repulsive skin disease which he treated by sitz baths. She left a note at his house saying that she had useful information for him from Normandy; hearing nothing from him, she sent a second note saying she would return for an interview in the evening. The date was July 13, 1793. She dressed in her best gown, inside which she had pinned a paper headed "Address to the French People," explaining the motives for her deed. Within the dress was also a kitchen knife with an ebony handle and a blade six inches long, which she had purchased that morning. The knife was in a cardboard sheath.

In the front hall the porter's wife, the cook, and Marat's mistress told her that it was impossible for her to see him. The sound of the raised voices reached Marat, who was preparing an issue of his paper in the bathroom. He asked for the caller to be brought in, since he realized that the names of the Girondists who were plotting his downfall in Normandy would be valuable in print. He received his visitor sitting in a high-walled copper bathtub which he had rented in the hope that soaking in it would help to cure the chronic skin ulcers from which he suffered. A plank had been placed across it to allow him to read and write.

Charlotte calmly answered his questions about the conspirators at Caen, while he took notes. After a very short time, his visitor in one swift movement took the knife from its sheath and plunged it between Marat's ribs into his heart. With only a single feeble cry for help, he died. The murderess was made a prisoner without a struggle; she made no attempt to escape. In an on-the-spot cross-examination by police officials Charlotte revealed the motives of her act: "Having seen civil war on the verge of blazing out all over France and persuaded that Marat was the principal author of this disaster, I preferred to make the sacrifice of my life in order to save my country."

The news spread quickly, and as she was taken to jail, only the greatest efforts of the police saved her from being torn to pieces by the infuriated mob along the route. Charlotte's trial was a mere formality. On July 19, six days after the murder, she was taken through the streets of Paris to the guillotine. On the platform her composure was unruffled, and her final statement was "I have killed one man in order to save a hundred thousand."

Marat became a martyr of the common people. Fifty thousand busts and statues of him were placed in the public parks during the next year. His death did not stop the Revolution. Persecution of the Girondists was increased, and even greater violence and unrest occurred under two other giants of the Revolution, Danton and Robespierre. One of the victims of the guillotine was Queen Marie Antoinette. The Terror, as it was called, lasted about a year, from the summer of 1793 through the summer of 1794; forty thousand were killed and 300,000 imprisoned. Peace was established only with the rise of Napoleon, ushering in a new era for France.

chapter eight

THE FUSE OF WORLD WAR I: SARAJEVO

Archduke Franz Ferdinand and his wife Sophie (June 28, 1914)

The Balkan states have always been the scene of much violence and murder. Assassinations have been common, and the struggles between the national minorities and their rulers go far back in modern history. In the geographical breakups arbitrarily arranged by the European dynasties, the unity of many ethnic groups was disregarded, and therein lay the seeds of discontent.

THE FUSE OF WORLD WAR I: SARAJEVO

The Austro-Hungarian Empire had been enlarged through the annexation of parts of many Balkan nations. When Franz Josef became Hapsburg Emperor in 1848, his empire was composed of many smaller nations. Others were added throughout his long, sixty-eight-year reign.

One of the satellites was Bosnia, which had been administered by Austria since 1878 and was annexed to it in 1908. Rebellions became common, for the Serbs and Croats, the principal national groups, resisted the take-over. It was to placate these groups and unify them that fifty-year-old Archduke FRANZ FERDINAND, nephew of Emperor Franz Josef and heir-apparent and future emperor, decided to make a visit to the provincial capital, Sarajevo, to express the interest and sympathy of the Hapsburgs in the internal problems of the Bosnians.

The archduke had married Countess SOPHIE CHOTEK in 1900. Since she was not of royal birth, she did not become an archduchess, and their three children had no royal rank. In his role as a field marshal and inspector general of the Austro-Hungarian Army, however, Franz Ferdinand was able to share public appearances with her at his side. The visit to Sarajevo on this fateful day was their fourteenth wedding anniversary.

The Slavic minorities in Bosnia—especially the youth—resented the fact that they had not been allowed to join Serbia, their national state. Many unsuccessful attempts had been made upon the lives of Hapsburg officials. When the archduke's visit was announced, a dozen students determined to shoot him, and they were encouraged in their plan by members of a Serb secret society, Union or Death, which gave them weapons.

After the archduke and his wife had observed Austrian army maneuvers in the Bosnian mountains, they motored to Sarajevo. The preparations for the visit included the omission of the military guard which normally lined the streets during an imperial visit; except for 150 policemen, the crowds were to have free access to their royal representative. This was intended as a gesture of friendship and peace.

Franz Ferdinand was dressed that day in the green uniform of an Austrian field marshal, with feathers waving from his military cap. As his six-car motorcade entered the town, he was in the open back seat of the second car with Sophie beside him. On the streets, he saw smiling faces and waving arms. As the procession approached the main part of the town, one of the boy conspirators failed to draw his revolver, another lost his courage and fled from his post, but a third threw a bomb at the royal car. His aim was inaccurate, and the bomb bounced off the rear of the automobile and exploded under the wheels of the car behind. The front tire blew out with a loud noise, spilling officers into the street. The unsuccessful assailant escaped down a nearby embankment where he was captured. He had swallowed cyanide which proved to be ineffective. The time was about 10:30 A.M.

One of the officers was bleeding, and Franz Ferdinand ordered the motorcade to stop. The automobile with the crumpled front wheel was quickly pushed off to the curb, and the remaining cars resumed their route, this time at a much faster pace. They were met at the city hall by the mayor, who commenced his address of welcome. The archduke furiously interrupted him.

"Mr. Mayor," he nearly shouted, "I came here on a visit and I get bombs thrown at me. It is outrageous!"

He then made a short speech, followed by a reception. As the royal party prepared to leave, Franz Ferdinand upbraided the provincial governor for the inadequate protection given his party and inquired somewhat sarcastically if there were likely to be more attempts to assassinate him during the remainder of his visit. The planned schedule was rearranged, and the archduke decided to visit the hospital where the wounded officers had been taken.

The chief of police and the deputy mayor took their places in the first car. A new automobile was brought up, and Franz and Sophie got in. An aide stood on the running board, and the motorcade started the trip, at greater speed than previously, along the embankment, following the morning's route in reverse. As the lead car reached the Latin Bridge, it turned off the embankment into a street originally scheduled in the itinerary for the party. Nobody had told the chauffeur that the route had been changed. The archduke's chauffeur blindly followed.

The provincial governor yelled to the driver, "Not that way, you fool! Keep straight on!" The rattled man stopped so that he could shift in reverse. Not two yards away stood a nineteen-year-old boy, Gavrilo Princip, with a loaded automatic pistol in his pocket. He had been discouraged that the previous attempt of his coconspirator had failed, but realized that a miraculous second chance had been offered by fate. The time was now 11:15 A.M.

He drew out his pistol and took careful aim. He could hardly have missed, since the range was ten feet. Princip fired twice. The first shot hit Franz Ferdinand, tearing through his chest and lodging against his spine. The second hit Sophie in the stomach, because she was trying to jump up and shield her husband with her body. For a few moments both of them continued to sit straight. Then, as the chauffeur finally got the car turned in the right direction and it leaped forward, the countess collapsed against the archduke. He remained upright, but a thin dark rivulet of blood stained the front of his tunic, and the corners of his mouth were red. He murmured "Sophie, Sophie! Don't die! Stay alive for our children!" His body slumped trying to brace the unconscious body of his wife. Fifteen minutes later, in a room next to where the waiters were preparing chilled champagne for his reception, the archduke died. His last words, repeated half a dozen times, were "It is nothing."

The successful assassin, Gavrilo Princip, had meanwhile been set upon by observers who tried to lynch him. He was beaten by the sword of one of the archduke's aides, and was seized by a detective while, intending to commit suicide, he managed to swallow poison. A bomb dropped to the pavement from his coat. He was arrested on the spot and taken to the police station for interrogation. Meanwhile, several accomplices had been apprehended.

At the trial of the twenty-two conspirators in October, Princip revealed the reasons for his act; they were typical of those given by most political assassins. "I am not a criminal," he told the court, "for I have suppressed a harmful man. . . . I am a South Slav nationalist. My aim is the union of all Slavs, under whatever political regime, and their liberation from Austria."

THE FUSE OF WORLD WAR I: SARAJEVO

"By what means did you think to accomplish that?" the judge asked.

"By terrorism" was the immediate answer.

The sentences were imposed on October 28, with the twenty-two prisoners chained in pairs. The leader of the conspiracy was given a life sentence and died in prison two years later. Three, including Princip, received twenty-year sentences at hard labor. Princip died of tuberculosis in 1918. Two received sixteen years, one thirteen, and one ten years. The sentences of five were death by hanging; three were executed; and two were reprieved, one commuted to life imprisonment and the other to a twenty-year prison term. Nine of the accused were set free. The prison sentences instead of death were pronounced because of the prisoners' youth.

Never was a statement more incorrect than the archduke's last words, "It is nothing." No other political murder in modern history has had such momentous consequences. One authority called the fatal discharge of Princip's pistol "the shots that still ring 'round the world."

The killing led to the outbreak of World War I by a series of quick and irreversible steps—the Austrian ultimatum to Serbia on July 23, her declaration of war on July 28, Russian mobilization, Germany's declaration of war on Russia on August 1, and French and British declarations of war against Germany on August 3 and 4.

The results have been simply stated by Vladimir Dediger in his stirring and comprehensive book, *The Road to Sarajevo:*

This four-year war produced the greatest carnage in world history up to that time, devastating much of Europe and causing the death of more than ten million people. Deep social upheavals followed it. The end came to four empires and the ancient Hapsburg, Romanov, Hohenzollern and Ottoman dynasties which had ruled them for hundreds of years. This war changed the map of Europe more than any previous war in its history; from the ruins of the former empires emerged new states based on the principle of self-determination. In Russia the 1917 revolution established an entirely new order. After 1918, Europe lost its decisive power over other parts of the world which it had subjugated in earlier centuries.

The two shots of nineteen-year-old Princip have been called "the perfect political murder" in the sense that it has been almost impossible for the truth regarding it to be established. The motives and the background instigators have never been fully clarified. The British Foreign Secretary in 1914, Sir Edward Grey, wrote in his postwar memoirs: "The world will presumably never be told all that was behind the assassination of the Archduke Franz Ferdinand. Probably there is not, and never was, any one person who knew all there was to know." Scholars and investigators are still uncovering new evidence that many governments, their public and secret agencies, and private political and clandestine organizations had an interest in eliminating the archduke. The full and complete truth has yet to be revealed.

chapter nine

VICTIMS OF THE RUSSIAN REVOLUTION

The story of the autocratic Russian rulers, particularly during the time when the lowly serfs began to find underground leaders who would fight for improvement of the conditions of their lives, is filled with scores of assassination attempts as well as successful murders. Terrorist activities were constant. When the Bolsheviks, later the Communist Party, began action toward the elimination of the monarchy, the peak of violence and killing was reached. This phase of Russia's history began during the lifetime and long rule of

Czar Nicholas II (1896–1917) and ended with the successful revolution of October, 1917.

THE END OF THE ROMANOV DYNASTY
Czar Nicholas II, Czarina Alexandra, four grand duchesses, Czarevitch Alexis, and four members of the household
(July 16, 1918)

Czar NICHOLAS II should have been aware of the discontent in his country, for his grandfather, one of his uncles, and three of his ministers, in addition to literally scores of government officials, were assassinated before the 1917 Bolshevik Revolution determined the fate of his own family.

In 1881, when Czarevitch Nicholas was thirteen years old, his grandfather, ALEXANDER II, the most liberal of Russia's nineteenth-century czars, who had freed the serfs, was killed by a bomb thrown under his carriage as he rode through the streets of St. Petersburg. Seven previous attempts had been unsuccessful. One of them, by a mine planted on the railway tracks near Moscow, was thwarted when Alexander took a train in another direction. Nicholas was present when his grandfather died. In 1905, during Nicholas' reign, one of his uncles, Grand Duke SERGE, governor-general of Moscow, was killed by a bomb dropped upon him from atop one of the Kremlin gates as he drove through.

During the early years of his reign, peasant and student terrorists were successful in attacks against his ministers and public officials. In 1901 an expelled university student shot and killed Nikolai BOGOLEPOV, the Minister of Education; the assassin became a hero of student demonstrations in St. Petersburg and Moscow. An attempt upon the life of Constantine Pobiedonostsev, the czar's former tutor, failed. In 1902 a student shot and killed Dimitri SIPIAGIN, the Minister of the Interior. An effort to kill a provincial governor failed; another succeeded. Two other governors were assassinated in 1904, as was Sipiagin's successor, Vyacheslav PLEHVE, Interior Minister, who was blown to pieces by a bomb. Plehve had been active in attempts to wipe out terrorist organizations, had conducted pogroms against the Jews, and was considered one of the most hated men in all Russia. Again, in 1911, Prime Minister Peter STOLYPIN was shot by a revolutionary during an opera performance in Kiev; he was sitting in the first row of the orchestra, and the act was witnessed by the Czar from his box near the stage. Stolypin, who died five days later, had also been active in putting down terrorism by terrorist tactics.

But Nicholas apparently was unmoved by these deaths as signs of the discontent of his people. He was, in fact, protected from knowledge of its extent, and apparently considered such hatred of the monarchy as an accepted part of his position. Terrorism was lawlessness, he reasoned, and the lawlessness and insubordination of his subjects must be suppressed even if drastic and extreme measures were called for.

Nicholas was basically a good family man, and very much attached to his wife ALEXANDRA, a granddaughter of Queen Victoria. His adoration of her, even when she was under the spell of Rasputin, was one of the weaknesses almost directly responsible for the end of the Romanov dynasty. Alexandra was the power behind the throne, and her influence upon Nicholas too often influenced his attitudes toward the policies of his ministers. Indeed, the gratitude of the Czar to Rasputin, the Mad Monk, for his effect on the health of the Czarevitch Alexis led him into unwise decisions taken in spite of the opposition of his advisers. Nicholas' gentleness was his prime weakness. He simply could not face the realities of his kingdom and its internal disturbances. The significance of the various revolts of workers and Bolsheviks escaped him completely. Though much constructive achievement marked his reign before World War I and a foundation of constitutional government was laid, the war was the beginning of the end of the monarchy. The revolutionary groups had previously been put down more or less successfully.

The country's participation in the war on the Allied side was catastrophic. Disasters in the offensive launched by Germany took a toll of lives and land; munitions and supplies were insufficient. To unite the people, Nicholas assumed the title and function of commander-in-chief. Political conflict between the Duma, or the legislative assembly, and the Czar became particularly dangerous, and the spread of defeatist doctrines opened the way for the forces of social revolution which had gone underground during the period of their suppression. The most active agents of Russia's defeat in the war were the Bolsheviks. In spite of the arrests, trials, and exiles of their leaders, plans were being made advocating a civil war of the lower classes against the higher classes to end the "imperialist" war.

Popular morale lowered with continued military and economic failures. The Bolsheviks acted swiftly and in March, 1917, launched the revolution by establishing a provisional government. On the second of March the Czar abdicated in favor of his brother, Grand Duke Michael, who refused the throne the next day. Nicholas made a trip to the army field headquarters to bid good-bye to his troops and returned to Petrograd to join his family, who were prisoners in one of the royal palaces. The family was promised safe conduct from Russia and were sent by special train to Tobolsk in Siberia. For a time the Czar hoped to escape in a royal yacht, but during the last week of April a special train took the Czar and Czarina to Ekaterinburg in the Ural Mountains, where their children joined them a few days later.

While the provisional government in Petrograd was attempting to placate the Bolsheviks to prevent further upheavals, efforts were being made to save the imperial family. A Bolshevik commissar, Vasily Yakovlev, was dispatched to bring Nicholas and Alexandra back to Moscow, but they were intercepted by local authorities when he took a westward route intending to cross the Ural Mountains. The royal couple were sent back to Ekaterinburg.

Germany took an interest in the matter in the belief that the restoration of the Russian monarchy and its crushing of the Bolsheviks would make the two countries friendly and stop the war on that front. Count Wilhelm von MIRBACH, the German ambassador to Russia, worked toward such an arrangement, but all hopes of success were blasted when he was assassinated early in July in his embassy in Moscow. His murderers were two Russian Social Revolutionaries who were convinced that Lenin and the Bolsheviks had betrayed the revolution to the Germans.

With all hopes of escape apparently vain, the royal family began a simple life in Ekaterinburg, their fates unknown. But plans were being formulated to dispose of them. The Bolshevik plan of conducting a "show" trial with a kangaroo court was thwarted by the advance from Siberia of a large Czech legion of 45,000 men who had become a part of the White Army. When they were within three days of Ekaterinburg, the Ural Soviet decided to shoot the entire family and dispose of their bodies.

Toward midnight of July 16, 1918, the entire family was summoned from their beds, and advised to dress quickly and go downstairs, on the pretext that automobiles were soon to arrive to move them. They were led to a small basement room. The group included, besides Nicholas and Alexandra and the Czarevitch ALEXIS, their four daughters—Grand Duchesses OLGA, TATIANA, MARIE, and ANASTASIA—the family doctor, the valet, the Czarina's maid, and the family cook. When they were all assembled, their executioner, Jacob Yurovsky, a member of the secret police, calmly announced that they were to be shot. Nicholas was killed instantly by a revolver fired at his head, followed by a hail of bullets from the squad, instantly killing all except Alexis and Anastasia. The maid, who survived the first volley, ran into the next room, where she was bayoneted more than thirty times. Still alive, the Czarevitch, lying in the arms of his father, feebly moved and was shot twice in the head by Yurovsky. Anastasia had fainted, but regained consciousness and screamed. With bayonets and rifle butts, the entire guard turned on her, and in a moment she lay still. The massacre was finished.

The bodies, wrapped in sheets, were transported by truck to a previously selected abandoned mine shaft fourteen miles away, where 150 gallons of gasoline and four hundred pounds of sulfuric acid had been deposited. Here the bodies were cut into pieces by axes and saws and then placed into huge bonfires. The remaining bones were dissolved in the acid, and the ashes and remains were thrown into the bottom of the mine shaft.

At first, announcement was made only that the Czar had been shot, and not until a year later did the Bolsheviks announce that the entire family was dead. To this day, however, rumors persist that Grand Duchess Anastasia escaped, and several claimants have appeared from time to time.

The Bolsheviks followed up their major crime by killing every member of the Romanov family on whom they could lay their hands. The czar's younger brother, Grand Duke MICHAEL, had been shot six days before Ekaterinburg. The day after the murder six other relatives were brutally murdered. Six months later four more grand dukes were executed in Petrograd.

The rule of the Romanovs was ended.

THE CZARINA'S FAVORITE
Gregory Rasputin (December 31, 1916)

Throughout history rulers and persons in power have often come under the spell of strong personalities who have influenced their actions and, in some cases, even controlled their lives. But none can compare with the Mad Monk who dominated the Russian Czarina Alexandra Feodorovna, and indirectly, her husband, Czar Nicholas II, to such an extent that he was a major contributor to the fall of the Romanov dynasty and even their eventual assassinations. From an obscure monk he became a self-styled "holy man" and gained such great power and influence over the rulers that they failed to heed the necessity for liberalizing their autocratic rule to respond to the demands of the majority peasant class and the Communists. His murder has been characterized as "one of the most grotesque episodes of twentieth-century history."

An illiterate peasant, he had been a student of hypnotism and mysticism before arriving in St. Petersburg in 1905, where he soon established a reputation as a miraculous healer. The Czarevitch Alexis, the only son of Alexandra and heir to the throne, had been born in 1904 and suffered from hereditary hemophilia. In 1912 when he had bruised himself and the court doctors had given up hope for his life and the last rites had been administered, the Czarina telegraphed to RASPUTIN, who was at his home in Siberia, begging him to pray for the life of her son. The monk cabled back, "God has seen your tears and heard your prayers. The little one will not die. Do not let the doctor bother him too much." Recovery was almost immediate, and Rasputin became a close associate of the royal family.

He soon gained complete control over Alexandra and, through her, over the Czar. The Czarina continued to call upon him to aid in healing her son through many attacks; she believed him to be an agent of God, since his healing powers were clearly a gift of the Almighty. His political power grew and his advice was accepted without question. The statesmen and ministers who tried to oppose him were removed from their posts; those who remained became his tools. The court was plunged into an almost insane atmosphere of mysticism, and the imperial family obeyed the slightest whims of the "holy man" even while Russia was suffering crushing defeats early in World War I. His many enemies came to realize that the only hope for survival of the monarchy lay in his death.

Two assassination attempts had failed. In 1914 Rasputin had been stabbed by a peasant woman in his Siberian hometown—on the same day as the assassination of Archduke Ferdinand at Sarajevo. In 1915, agents of a rival monk attempted unsuccessfully to kill him with a horse-drawn sled by running him down. The leader of the final conspiracy was Prince Felix Youssoupov, who was married to a niece of the Czar. He had met the monk several times, and Rasputin had even suggested to him that Nicholas should abdicate in favor of Alexis, with the Czarina installed as regent. Convinced that Rasputin's presence was destroying the monarchy, he joined with four friends in concocting a plot. The murder would take place in the cellar of Youssoupov's Moika Palace, where he would feed Rasputin poison. The others would later take charge of removing the body. Accordingly, the prince invited the monk to a midnight party. Encouraged by the assurance that Irina, the wife of the prince, would be present, Rasputin readily accepted the invitation.

Never was a murder more difficult. First the prince offered chocolates, almond cakes, and Madeira wine, all laced with enough potassium cyanide "to kill several men instantly." At first the monk refused the cakes, but finally began to eat and to drink, while the prince entertained him by singing and playing the guitar. Once Rasputin's eyes closed, but when the song ended, he demanded another. This went on for two and a half hours, while the coconspirators paced feverishly upstairs, listening to a phonograph record of "Yankee Doodle" played repeatedly—this was to indicate that a party was being given by Princess Irina, who was actually absent in Crimea.

In desperation the prince finally pulled out a pistol and fired twice at Rasputin's heart. The monk fell, "gasping and roaring like a wounded animal." But as Youssoupov leaned over him, Rasputin seized him by the throat and tore an epaulet from his shoulder. The prince fled upstairs, with Rasputin, bleeding and bellowing, in pursuit on all fours. The rest was pure nightmare.

In the snow-covered courtyard, one of the conspirators fired two more shots into Rasputin, then kicked him in the head as he fell. Youssoupov, retching and half-crazed, leaped on the prostrate monk and beat him with a steel bar. He then noticed one eye still open and collapsed in the arms of his servants, while the other plotters carried off the monk's bound body and threw it into the icy Neva River, where it was found two days later.

The power of the Mad Monk thus ended, but two years later his benefactors were to be cruelly done away with.

ONE OF THE REVOLUTION'S LEADERS
Leon Trotsky (August 20, 1940)

The French Revolution and the Russian Revolution of 1917 both represented fundamental alterations in social, political, and economic structures, and in every way are classic examples of revolution. Through the overthrow of long-established monarchies, entirely new concepts of government and national life came into existence. Both came at critical moments which aided the revolutionaries.

In March, 1917, power in Russia was seized by a series of short-lived, weak governments, the best known of which was that of Kerensky. The Bolshevik leaders—Lenin, Trotsky, and Stalin—were all out of the country. But by October it was possible for the Bolsheviks to take over the revolution and along with it final power and authority. Violence and terror, of course, were common as effective tools. The complicated maneuvers involved in the 1917 seizure of power need not be outlined here, for of the many murders and assassinations that resulted, we are concerned with only two—the Czar and his family, and one of the most powerful leaders, Leon TROTSKY, born as Lev Bronstein in 1877.

A Marxist revolutionist by the time he was twenty-one, Trotsky was several times arrested and exiled for his activities as a propagandist, agitator, and journalist. But always he returned to Russia, often by underground routes, to pursue his career. In Germany at the beginning of World War I, he was imprisoned for his freely expressed antiwar views. He was expelled from France in 1916 and spent the next six months in the United States. After the March Revolution he returned to Russia, where he joined Lenin, helped to stage the October Revolution, and rapidly rose to power. As people's commissar for foreign affairs under Lenin, he negotiated peace with Germany in the treaty of Brest-Litovsk. Then, as War Commissar, he organized the victorious Red Army in the Civil War of 1918–20. He was not involved in the murder of the royal family, since he was absent at the front when it took place. He had, nevertheless, proposed a public "show" trial to be broadcast throughout the country, and he expressed his opinion of the assassination in the following words: "The execution was needed not only to frighten, horrify, and dishearten the enemy, but also in order to shake up our ranks to show that there was no turning back, that ahead lay either complete victory or complete ruin."

His difficulties began in 1924 after Lenin's death, when he organized the leftist opposition against Stalin. Since the Central Committee of the Communist Party, the Politburo, could not countenance any criticism or deviation from the majority, Trotsky was expelled in November, 1927. He was first exiled to a southern village, then deported from Russia to Turkey. He became a wanderer, finding asylum in Turkey, France, and Norway. The Soviet government obtained his expulsion from the latter country in 1937 after Trotsky's name had been linked, somewhat recklessly and inaccurately, with vast plots against Stalin in the Moscow treason trials of the 1930's, the party purge. He and his son LEON were in absentia sentenced to death. Trotsky not only denied these charges but hurled countercharges at Stalin, many of them highly damaging and embarrassing. In 1938 his son was murdered in Paris.

From that time on, Trotsky was a marked man, for he knew from his own experience as a terrorist and party member that deviators from the party line and criticizers of any of the leaders were intolerable and must be punished. Death was inevitable. However, after he settled in Coyocan, a suburb of Mexico City, in 1937, he found a degree of contentment half a world away from the center of Communist power.

His life in Mexico was quiet and peaceful, and he continued his writing, which included what would be, he hoped, the definitive and true life of dictator Stalin. Under heavy guard at all times behind the walls surrounding his home, haunted by the specter of death at the hands of some member of the NKVD, the Soviet political police, Trotsky felt that he would eventually be disposed of, in accordance with the 1936 death sentence. He became accustomed to living in the shadow of impending assassination, almost abandoning all hope of escaping Stalin's murder machine. Followers and sympathizers in the United States raised several thousand dollars to transform his villa into a virtual fortress; twenty-foot walls were built, and a special wing was constructed with bomb-proof ceilings and floors. Double steel doors, controlled by electric switches, replaced the former wooden entrance. Three new bulletproof towers were erected to serve as observation points. The Mexican government supplied police guards around the clock, and an inner guard made up of tough men from the American Teamsters' Union were on duty day and night. Trotsky lived like a cloistered prisoner.

The first attempt was made on May 24, 1940. Early that morning, a twenty-man force of plotters wearing Mexican army and police uniforms and armed with submachine guns and bombs converged on Trotsky's home after beating and trussing the policeman on the street. The men then cut the telephone lines running into the house and the secret electric line leading to local police headquarters. At the entrance one of the men pulled the bell cord, and the guard, in disobedience of the established procedure, opened the door fully instead of a few inches. He was seized. The entire attacking force swarmed inside and broke into detachments. One raider fired a hail of bullets into the rear guardhouse, immobilizing the five men sleeping there.

The main group meanwhile proceeded directly toward the two bedrooms of the house, where they knew the Trotskys and their grandson slept. With murderous submachine gunfire, they shot through both the windows and doors. Trotsky and his wife threw themselves on the floor and sought shelter under a bed. Since they apparently knew that there was a device on the door which, once it was set, fired automatically on anyone who tried to cross the threshold, the attackers did not attempt to enter. Instead, they placed an incendiary bomb at the door. The door and floor boards started to burn. This was for the purpose of destroying the house and Trotsky's Communist Party records, including the manuscript of the Stalin biography. A final burst of automatic fire was centered on the beds before the assailants left. Their four automobiles were abandoned not far from the scene of the attack, and the gate guard was killed. The Trotskys had almost miraculously escaped by remaining on the floor throughout the episode.

The leader was eventually exposed as David Siqueiros, a Mexican Communist and painter, who was tried, by a twist of the Mexican law, only for housebreaking. Though three hundred bullets had been fired, he maintained that the foray had been made only for "psychological purposes"; he had no intention, he said, of killing or hurting anybody. He jumped bail and found asylum in Chile. When he was extradited to Mexico, he was warmly welcomed and was never brought to trial.

From the day of this attack, Trotsky knew that he was no longer safe. It was only a question of time. His assassin struck on August 20, 1940. He went under the name of "Frank Jacson"; his real name was Ramón Mercader, and he had been a Spanish Communist and officer during the Civil War in Spain. He had come to Mexico shortly after the unsuccessful attempt under the sponsorship and financial support of the NKVD with the assigned mission of infiltrating the Trotsky household as a preliminary to his act. Posing as an engineer, he made friends with several of the guards, through whom he gained an intimate knowledge of the premises and the habits and movements of Trotsky himself. He even drove Mrs. Trotsky on a trip to Veracruz. Several times he later dined with the family. After he had made many reports on Trotsky's life and activities to Moscow, he was summoned to New York City in June, 1940, and briefed thoroughly by the resident NKVD representative attached to the Soviet consulate general. He was given a large sum of money to finance both the assassination and his anticipated escape from the scene of the crime.

Back in Cocoyan, he continued to be welcome to the Trotsky household, all the time observing the surroundings in which he would carry out his assignment. When the time came, he was fully prepared. The purpose of his visit that day was to submit a manuscript to Trotsky for criticism. This would serve as a pretext for entering the study and being alone with his victim. Inside one coat pocket Jacson carried a dagger 13¾ inches long. In the other pocket he had an ice ax with a small cut-down handle; its head was about seven inches long, and the blade had been sharpened. In his back trousers' pocket he carried the third weapon, an automatic pistol with eight bullets in the magazine and one in the firing chamber. He was thus prepared for any situation and opportunity. All preparations were made for the successive steps in his act and for his successful escape.

After tea with the Trotskys at about five o'clock, Jacson asked Trotsky for criticism of his manuscript, and together they went to the study, Jacson still holding his raincoat. Trotsky sat down at his cluttered desk and began reading the manuscript. Jacson leaned over his shoulder. From his coat he removed the heavy Alpine ice ax, and struck Trotsky's skull a blow which proved ineffective for the kill. Leaping from his chair, Trotsky grappled with his assailant, biting his hand. He staggered, screaming, into the dining room, where bodyguards clubbed Jacson, knocked him down, and kicked his head and body. Trotsky collapsed on the floor, blood streaming from his broken skull, and called to the guard, "Don't kill him. This man Jacson has a story to tell!"

Although his skull was fractured and his brain pierced, Trotsky clung to consciousness in the hospital for more than twenty-five hours before he died after two brain operations. His ashes were buried in Paris.

Under his true name of Ramón Mercader, the assassin was brought to trial and sentenced to twenty years' imprisonment in 1943, a period which he served.

chapter ten

VIOLENT DEATH OF A NONVIOLENT LEADER

Mahatma Gandhi (January 30, 1948)

The path of the good, unselfish, and dedicated man throughout history has never been easy. The leader whose cause is worthy invariably meets powerful opposition from those who seek to destroy him, if necessary by violent means. He becomes a controversial figure, and must live in fear of his life.

Mahatma GANDHI—the term "Mahatma" means "great soul" in Sanskrit, and in India designates a person who is held in the highest esteem for his wisdom and saintliness—is invariably mentioned in lists of the most admired men in modern history.

The multifaceted personality of Gandhi was the most extraordinary thing about him. He was a spiritual guide and leader, a politician, a lover of all mankind, a man of action and deeds, fearlessly devoted to his beliefs. As a politician heading the Indian Congress Party, he probably did more to achieve Indian independence than any other single figure. A visionary, he had a highly practical side. He recognized the barriers confronting him, and attempted, not always successfully, to hurdle them. His patience and perseverance were continually evident. The term "a truly good man" is not enough, for he was saintly as well, and there is a great difference. Inevitably he encountered almost overwhelming opposition, but his faith in spiritual persuasion never failed him. The term "charisma" is of wide current usage; it is defined as "that special spiritual power or personal quality that gives an individual influence or authority over large numbers of people, worthy of veneration." This fits Gandhi perfectly. He was the man for the times in India.

The gem of the British Empire, India was one of its proudest colonies. A composite of many races and religions, with native customs difficult for Westerners to understand, India was never complacent under British rule. From time to time revolts and internal strife erupted, always to be put down by the masters. Assassination was uncommon because the Indians are basically a gentle people. The main official victim was Viceroy Richard Bourke, the EARL OF MAYO, who in 1872 was stabbed twice by an assailant who had served a sentence for murder. For three years this man had planned the act, and when he was asked at his trial why he had committed the murder, he only replied, "By the order of God." To the question of whether he had any associates in his act, he answered, "Among men I have no accomplice; God is my partner." He was hanged.

Gandhi's life and acts have been the subject of many books and cannot be discussed herein in detail. His unique method was the technique of nonviolence, sometimes called passive resistance. While imprisoned in Cape Colony, South Africa, in 1908 for leading nonviolent protests against the exclusion of Indians from the state of Transvaal as immigrants, Gandhi read a lecture by Henry David Thoreau titled "The Rights and Duties of the Individual in Relation to Government," printed in 1849 under the changed title "Civil Disobedience."

Thoreau's idea was that an individual, to protect his own integrity, was justified in not obeying laws of which he did not morally approve. He might not be successful, but his resistance could eventually change the laws; at least the individual's noncooperation could serve to call attention to the flaws. Although Thoreau's theory of noncooperation was an individual one, Gandhi's was collective, as a means of mass protest. The Mahatma coined the word *satyagraha,* literally translated as "truth force" but meaning struggle without violence.

For twenty-eight years Gandhi conducted his campaign against British rule and for the independence of India. In every phase of native life, his followers conducted such protests. One of its prime features was that civil disobedience would often, almost invariably, lead to arrest and imprisonment, a penalty which was anticipated and readily accepted.

He was arrested scores of times, always to return to preaching his gospel. From time to time he agreed to halt civil disobedience, only to begin again when the conditions were not honored. He instituted countless boycotts, most of them successful. He used personal means to stimulate his followers and to show his dedication. He fasted not only for religious and personal reasons but also in a public cause. As one writer has expressed it, "The fast was an adventure in goodness. The stake was one man's life. The prize was the nation's freedom."

Gandhi was a complicated puzzle to the British overlords, but the menial, undernourished, miserable, exploited masses understood both his methods and his purposes. No obstacle was too great to overcome, and the periodic losses and bad times never discouraged him. In failure he seemed to renew his strength for further battles.

The aim to which Gandhi had dedicated his life was achieved when, on August 15, 1947, the viceroy, Lord Louis Mountbatten, announced that all British officials would leave India, and that two hundred years of subjection to foreign rule had ended. In his speech, the viceroy reminded his audience that to no one did the country owe its independence so much as to Mahatma Gandhi.

The great leader was not present; he was far away praying for his people and peace. A fanatical uprising revolving around the new state of Pakistan resulted in an orgy of murder and destruction. Though independence had been gained, Gandhi was deeply grieved because his ideal of brotherhood had apparently failed. As a penance he began a fast in New Delhi on January 13, 1948, thus hoping to heal the wounds of disunity. His weight had fallen to 107 pounds, and the

VIOLENT DEATH OF A NONVIOLENT LEADER

fast brought results, a pledge of peace. A handmade bomb had been thrown at him from the nearby garden wall but had exploded beyond his range.

On the evening of January 30, he went to the prayer ground on the estate where he was staying. Just as he was touching his palms together in the traditional Hindu greeting to those assembled, a man elbowed his way through the crowd and, planting himself about two feet in front of Gandhi, fired three shots from an automatic pistol. As the first bullet struck him, he faltered. The second bullet struck; blood began to stain his white robes. His face turned pale. The Mahatma murmured, *"Hey, Rama* (oh, God)." A third shot rang out, and the limp body fell to the ground. His spectacles dropped to the earth, and the leather sandals slipped from his feet. Two of the bullets had passed completely through his body, the third embedded itself in the lung. In accordance with Hindu custom, the body was burned the next day on a funeral pyre. Close to a million people were present. A fortnight later the ashes were thrown into rivers throughout India as prescribed by Hindu ritual.

The assassin was Nathuram Godse, a Hindu. He and the eight others who had bombed the house several days before were tried together. Godse admitted that he felt the Pakistan unrest could never be calmed as long as Gandhi lived.

In 1968 the twentieth anniversary of his death was officially observed. The Indian government announced that the grounds of the New Delhi house where the great leader was assassinated would become a national monument.

Though his activities were localized, Mahatma Gandhi had in an extraordinary way affected people throughout the world, and seldom has a public figure received more tributes. Prime Minister Nehru was speaking for his own country when he said, "The light has gone out of our lives, and there is darkness everywhere," but the statement regarding this unparalleled "fighter without a sword" might appropriately have been made for people of good will everywhere.

chapter eleven

THE MIDDLE EAST

The collective term "Middle East" generally includes all the nations from the eastern shores of the Mediterranean and Aegean Seas from Turkey to India, including the countries of southwest Asia and often Egypt: Turkey, Syria, Lebanon, Israel, Jordan, Iraq, Iran, and Saudi Arabia. Many of the present country names have been adopted during the past four decades. Israel was Palestine until 1948; Jordan, the full name of which is the Hashemite Kingdom of Jordan, was Transjordan until 1949; Iraq was Mesopotamia until 1932; and Iran was Persia until 1935.

The liberation of these countries was due for the most part to nationalist movements from within. Political assassination has been an integral part of their development. Only the contemporary murders which have caused major changes in governments, with a few exceptions, can be discussed in the following sections.

These nations formed the cradle of civilization and have experienced a longer history than any others. They have been magnets for would-be conquerors. The internal struggles involved in the independence movements and the attempted modernization of various countries have caused the assassinations described in this chapter. The Arab-Jewish struggle, for example, was responsible for the two in Palestine in pre-Israel days. The Middle East has been termed the most explosive part of the contemporary world because of the growth of intense nationalism and the resistance of elements in the countries to modernization.

IRAN

In the eleventh century, Persia's secret sect of Hashasheen gave the world a new word for political murder—assassination. The ancient tradition of treating politics as a matter of life and death still survives. Political parties were banned by the ruling Shah until 1941, but loosely organized and secret societies always flourished. Some of the more recent organizations have been strongly nationalistic and extremist.

The major cause of current discontent in Iran has been opposition to Shah Mohammed Reza Pahlevi's White Revolution, so-called because he hopes to implement it without bloodshed. In a desperate and dedicated effort to modernize his country, he has introduced far-reaching reforms to benefit his subjects. Among other changes, land redistribution to peasants and women's rights have been introduced. In pressing for these advances, he has made many enemies who would welcome his fall.

The present Shah, who came to the throne in 1941, possesses extensive powers, granted in the country's 1906 constitution and its many amendments. He rules by the "grace of God"; the executive power is wholly in his hands, and he is vested with the right of delaying legislation passed by parliament. This has rendered him more than ordinarily susceptible to violent opposition, and resistance to his determined policies has been continuous.

Several attempts have been made on his life. The Shah dodged bullets in 1949 when a man disguised as a photographer fired upon him with a pistol: one bullet grazed his lip, another pierced his military cap, and the third ripped off an epaulet. Again in 1965, after Premier Mansour had been assassinated, a young soldier of his own Imperial Guard attempted to kill the Shah with an automatic machine gun, but the series of eight shots hit another guard who ran to protect the ruler. Before dying, the guard sent a burst from his own gun into the assailant and killed him.

The foiling of this assassination attempt was considered a great blessing for Iran, for, as one official stated, "If the Shah should die, this country would be reduced to chaos." Young Crown Prince Reza was only four years old and could not have held effective power even through a regent. This attempt caused a temporary reaction against the extremist groups and aided the Shah's popular image.

In modern times one Shah, NASR-ED-DIN, who ruled for

forty-eight years, was shot as he was entering a shrine near Teheran by a member of a seditious sect that had been banished from Persia five years before. The Shah had attempted to modernize his country with ideas he had gained from three extensive tours throughout Europe. His son, Mussafer-ed-din, who succeeded him, narrowly escaped assassination in 1900 near Paris while on a trip visiting the French capital.

Premier AMIN-ES-SULTAN, who held that post three times, was shot and killed as he was leaving the Parliament building on August 31, 1907. His assailant, a banker, immediately killed himself after stabbing a soldier who attempted to arrest him. On his body were found four capsules of strychnine, a piece of caustic, and a card identifying him as a member of a political society or *anjuman*. The adjective applied to the name was "self-devoted," the term originally applied to the Hashasheen who carried out the orders of the Old Man of the Mountain. This particular body of the *anjuman* numbered forty members, all dedicated to murder for the traditional purpose. In this case, the assassin, Abbas Aqa, was venerated as a patriot who had given his life to rid his country of a traitor. Over 100,000 admirers gathered to visit his tomb forty days after his death. The tributes paid to him include an elegy written at the time, illustrating how a typical political assassin's act may be glorified:

> O Abbas, O Courage incarnate, who, guided by honor,
> Sawest thy country sore wounded, and laid healing ointment on her!

The next major assassination was that of Premier Ali RAZMARA, on whom the Western powers had staked their hopes. On March 7, 1951, while in a mosque, he was shot by a member of an extremist group of fanatics numbering at most a few thousand, whose newspaper promptly and openly boasted of their responsibility for the crime. The particular incitement to the act was that the Premier had publicly rejected as impracticable the demand to nationalize the Anglo-Iranian Oil Company's concession, a major foreign investment contributing great sums to the state. The assassin, Khalil Tahmasabi, overnight became a national hero and made this statement: "If I have rendered a humble service, it was for the Almighty in order to deliver the deprived Muslim people of Iran from foreign serfdom." So bitter was the feeling toward the Shah at this time that he was forced to slip out of the country and go to Italy. While he was absent, pitched battles were fought in streets of the capital between his enemies and his supporters, and the nationalization of the oil company was immediately legislated. The fanatics responsible for Razmara's death subsequently assassinated the vice-chancellor of Teheran University and attempted unsuccessfully to murder the local governor.

The internal turmoil persisted, and the Shah's policies of modernization were strongly opposed by both ultraconservative Muslims and the feudal landowners. The most recent major assassination was that of Premier Hassan Ali MANSOUR in January, 1965. When his official limousine reached the entrance to the Iranian Parliament building in Teheran, his bodyguard jumped from the front seat, two doormen rushed forward, and army guards snapped to attention. As the Premier got out of the car, pistol shots rang out, and Mansour clutched his throat and fell to the wet pavement, blood streaming through his fingers. One of the doormen whipped around and knocked a smoking revolver from the hand of a Muslim student who was seized by other guards. Later, police rounded up two more young Muslims as the boy's accomplices; on their pistols were pasted the slogan "Down with the undemocratic regime of the Shah." Mansour survived for five days after surgeons had taken two bullets from his throat and stomach and removed part of his intestine. The assassination was not carried out for personal reasons, for like most Iranian premiers before him, Mansour was never much more than an instrument employed by the Shah in putting his plans and hopes for his country into action.

Undaunted by the opposition, which often takes the form of violent protests and riots, Shah Mohammed Reza Pahlevi, one of the few Arab heads of state who is a staunch friend of the West, continues his efforts to improve the living conditions of his people.

IRAQ

Before 1932, this country was called Mesopotamia, and its history in the Tigris-Euphrates Valley dates as far back as 3000 B.C. In modern times it was a Turkish possession, but after World War I was mandated by the League of Nations to Great Britain and became a sovereign state in 1932. The constitutional monarchy was set up in 1924. The first King, Faisal I, died in 1933. His eldest son ruled for a short period, and was succeeded in 1939 by FAISAL II, who was then four years old. For fourteen years he ruled under the regency of his uncle Crown Prince Abdul ILLAH, and they were both assassinated in 1958.

The country has been long divided, with strong Arab anti-Jewish sentiments, but Iraq is also allied with Jordan in opposition to Egypt. Strong Arab nationalists, antimonarchists, and anti-Western groups held the country in turmoil which culminated in a successful military coup on July 14, 1958. Overnight the monarchy was abolished, and the pro-Western regime was wiped out. The King, the crown prince, the Premier, and more than two hundred others were killed, and a republic was declared.

This army coup provides an excellent example of the employment of assassination for political purposes. The plot had been well planned by General Abdul Karim Kassem and was carried out with brutal ferocity. Twenty-three-year-old Faisal II was shaving at dawn on July 14, when soldiers broke past the gates of the royal palace in Baghdad. Outside, a mob had already set the building afire, and smoke drove the King down into the courtyard where the soldiers and crowd were waiting. Crown Prince Abdul Illah ordered the palace guard to open fire and reached for his own pistol. Guns blazed on both sides, and both the King and his uncle fell, fatally wounded. The King's body was bundled into a rug and spirited away, presumably because he was felt to be the tool of his Premier, Nuri-es-Said and thus not as guilty. The dead body of the crown prince, however, was hanged as a public display by the mobs at least twice that day. Between the hangings it was constantly stoned and parts of his body were cut off and carried away as souvenirs. Seventeen of the King's guards had also been murdered in the palace courtyard.

Baghdad was in turmoil. Unruly mobs roamed the streets, attacking and sacking public buildings in an orgy of fury and violence. The military leaders seized the key government buildings, telephone, telegraph, and radio centers with no opposition. The British embassy was ransacked and burned, and two American businessmen were killed by a crowd that stormed the new Baghdad Hotel.

The principal target of the revolutionists was not immediately found. Seventy-year-old NURI-ES-SAID had held the post of Premier seventeen times in thirty-seven years and had been friendly to the British. As a shrewd and powerful politician, he had cemented relations with both Great Britain and the United States. His attempts to establish and maintain a democratic government had been met with uninterrupted opposition—the revolt's leader, General Kassem, later boasted that the plan had been hatched fifteen years earlier and only awaited "the proper time" to be put into action—but the Premier had almost miraculously survived as the number-one strong man of Iraq, for the King was only a figurehead. On this fateful morning Nuri-es-Said escaped from his house and was not discovered until the afternoon. He and two subofficials, disguised as veiled women in black coats, were walking along a main street seeking a refuge, when a man in the crowd noticed men's shoes and the bottoms of pajama pants below the long coat of one of them. He jerked open the coat and identified the Premier as "Nuri!" Thus unmasked, Nuri wearily confessed, "I am the pasha. I am sick." As he turned to run, the cry of the mob alerted a passing driver who jumped the curb with his auto and pinned their target against a wall. Nuri was shot and killed by an air-force sergeant. His body was then attacked again and again, was stabbed and stomped upon until an army vehicle arrived, rescued what remained, and took it to a hospital. That night the Premier's body was secretly buried in a cemetery, but the next morning mobs disinterred his remains from the fresh grave and hung it naked on public exhibition, where it was stoned, sliced for souvenirs, and several times taken down and dragged behind automobiles. The body of his son, who was killed with him, had been dragged through the streets the day before by a mob waving knives and shouting, "Freedom!"

The death toll was a surprisingly low total of thirty; the revolt had succeeded almost immediately because the resentment of nationalists against the government had festered so long that the mobs, when given the signal, aided the military in the successful coup.

The new Premier, General Abdul Karim KASSEM, soon welcomed the Communists, whose party had been outlawed by Nuri-es-Said. Steps were taken toward allying more closely with Nasser and the United Arab Republic, but a split soon occurred. During his four and a half years in power, twenty-nine plots were uncovered and twelve attempts upon his life failed. His closest call came in 1959, when his automobile was ambushed, and he spent fifty days in a hospital. These assailants were pro-Nasserites, and thereafter Kassem always rode in a bulletproof car and slept in the defense ministry.

Early in 1963, the general dismissed fifty-eight Iraqi generals and replaced them with pro-Communists. During a coup staged by young officers on February 8, both the presidential palace and the defense ministry were air-bombed. Kassem was found in the ruins of the ministry with three aides, and was assassinated. The bodies, in the positions of death, were pictured on national television to show the people that the Communist domination of the country had ended. Guilt was fixed on agents of the United Arab Republic. Since that time successive military governments have been in power, frequently changing through bloody coups. The strong ties with Nasser have continued; Iraq is the sworn enemy of Jordan, Iran, and Israel in the current power struggle in the Middle East.

JORDAN

An ancient land in existence since biblical times, this tiny nation was a part of the Ottoman Empire from the sixteenth century until World War I, after which it was mandated to the British and became known as Transjordan, an independent country, in 1923. The British sponsorship continued, however, and full independence was granted in 1946 when the name was changed to the Hashemite Kingdom of Jordan, and Emir Abdullah's title was changed to King.

Abdullah was a shrewd and realistic politician whose principal object was the winning of Arab independence and the building up of the Arab nations. When the British decided to withdraw from Palestine in 1948, the other Arab countries, with their strong anti-Jewish feelings, embarked on an unsuccessful war with the new state of Israel. The defeated nations resented Abdullah because he was friendly to the Jewish state and had close relations with it. Half of his kingdom, on the west bank of the Jordan, adjoined Israel, and the former Palestinian Arabs became Jordanian citizens. Hatred of him among the other Arab nations was generated by Egypt, and he was denounced as a friend of the Jews, the enemy of the Arabs, and under the domination of Great Britain, "the imperialists." He was also charged by Arab nationalists as being too friendly to the West.

On July 20, 1951, King ABDULLAH visited the Aqsa Mosque in the Old City of Jerusalem, on his weekly pilgrimage to honor the prophet Muhammad, from whom he was a thirty-nine-generation direct descendant. He was accompanied by his grandson, fifteen-year-old Emir Hussein. As he was slipping off his shoes preparatory to joining four thousand other Muslims at prayer, he was fired at by a young Arab tailor in Western clothes who was hidden behind the door. Five bullets from an American automatic struck his face and chest. Five accomplices of the assassin simultaneously fired into the roof of the mosque, and the crowd of worshipers stampeded. Abdullah's body was trampled in the panicky rush. The accomplices escaped, but the killer placed the gun to his right temple and shot himself. The guards of the King rushed in; they fired crazily, clubbed with their guns and stabbed with their bayonets, killing at least twenty. A stray bullet tore a medal off the tunic of Emir Hussein, who, instead of rushing for cover, chased the assassin before being stopped and spirited away.

The present ferment in the Middle East has been attributed to Abdullah's death, since he was the only moderate among the nations, and with him expired all hopes of achieving any sort of an alliance of Jordan, Syria, and Lebanon as pro-Western allies. Thereafter, Jordan was torn between the pro-West and the Arab states.

Abdullah's son and successor, Talal, was judged insane a year later, and Hussein became the world's youngest King upon coming of age in 1953. He has lived in constant danger from the vengeful Palestinian Arabs in his kingdom. During the first year of his reign, an assassination plot engineered by Nasser was uncovered. Plots against him and his throne have been frequent. Once, while he was crossing Syria en route to Europe, two Syrian jets swooped down close to the plane bearing him and made an additional five forays against him before the King reached the Jordanian capital of Amman in safety. Though he has constantly attempted to effect caution among other Arab leaders in their conflict over Israel, his life is in perpetual danger, and he always moves under a heavy security guard. Jordan has been rightly termed "an assassination powder keg."

The only other major assassination in the Hashemite Kingdom was the murder of Hussein's first Premier, Hazzah MAJALI, on August 29, 1960. It was his custom to grant a weekly audience for the public, and in his office on the second floor of the foreign ministry on that morning, a huge bomb burst in his desk drawer, killing him instantly. Almost immediately a second bomb exploded. The total casualties were eleven dead and forty-three wounded. The plot was traced to the United Arab Republic's President, Abdul Nasser; previous plots against Majali had been uncovered in March and again in May. Two minor Jordanian government employees who had escaped to Syria were returned for trial and later executed, and fourteen others were found to be involved. The bombs had been delivered to an Amman bookshop in a package labeled "press material." The two messengers had taken them into the office building in a suitcase the night before and set fuses. Majali's "crime" had been that he was trying to improve Jordan's relations with the West. This ended the country's brief association with the

United Arab Republic and encouraged Hussein's continued suspicion of other Arab nations with whom he could not see eye to eye. Since then, the King has been increasingly a loner in the morass of Arab politics.

OTHER ARAB COUNTRIES

Several other Middle Eastern countries have also had their share of political assassinations during the period of post-World War II unrest in the Middle East. Six major murders occurred between 1948 and the assassination of King Abdullah of Jordan in 1951. In the Middle Eastern world there are fifty million Muslims. These nations have several common fears which have resulted in turmoil and the murders of prominent leaders. These common problems are: hatred of the Jews; political leaders eager to exploit nationalist ambitions; resentment of Western dominance in natural resources, particularly oil; suspicion of outside economic and political interests; and resistance to proposals for the unification of Arab countries. Each Muslim nation has a minority of religious fanatics who, following the tradition of the Hashasheens, believe that the murder of anyone opposing them or of whose actions they disapprove is blessed by Allah.

Count Folke BERNADOTTE was the first major figure to be killed during this period of hatred, ambition, and intrigue. As United Nations mediator for Palestine, he had the mission of trying to bring together Jews and Arabs. He was shot to death on September 17, 1948, by members of Israel's Stern Gang. Three months later in Cairo an organization of zealots, the Muslim Brothers, killed the Premier of Egypt, Mahmoud Fahmy EL NOKRASHY. The leader of the plot was seized later in a gun battle and was executed; his accomplices were jailed for life. Before the execution, the Muslim Brothers threatened to kidnap Nokrashy's children if the sentence were carried out. This political party, the largest in Egypt, was dedicated to stemming the tide of Westernization; its leader, Sheikh Hassen al-BANNA, was assassinated in 1949, but the party continued its activities, even attempting unsuccessfully to murder President Nasser in 1954.

Syria's chief assassination, in 1949, was that of President (Colonel) Husni ZAIM who had led a successful army coup d'etat. He had been in power only from March to August when he was shot by the same army men who had helped him seize power. His offense was to introduce many social reforms, including women's rights.

Lebanon's major casualty was Premier Riad es-SOHL, who had sought to bring Muslims and Christians together by a national pact which proclaimed the brotherhood of all Lebanese of whatever sect. In July of 1951 he was in Amman, Jordan, conferring with King Abdullah on his plan to unite his country with Syria to form an Arab superstate, a proposal which the Jordan King opposed. After the conference he started for the airport with a police escort provided by his host. En route he was murdered by a burst of bullets from a tommy gun fired from a passing car. The killers proved to be two members of the Syrian National Party, who opposed the plan. One of the men was shot by the bodyguards, and the other committed suicide on the spot. Rioting broke out in Lebanon's capital, Beirut, where angry bands roamed the streets smashing store windows. When es-Sohl's body arrived home by plane, screaming mobs ripped off the door, seized the coffin and carried it to his home, continuously crying out loudly against Abdullah. In May, 1968, Lebanon's ex-President Camille CHAMOUN was shot and killed by a member of a left-wing group who claimed Chamoun was planning to push neutral Lebanon into the Western camp. He was hit by four bullets in both arms and the face, and the assailant was immediately killed by Chamoun's bodyguards.

The wave of assassinations during the 1950's and 1960's continues unabated, and political murders may be expected to occur in the future.

PALESTINE

After World War I, Palestine was a land of turmoil, both political and racial. It became a British mandate at that time along with Iraq, then called Mesopotamia. One of the articles of the mandate, upholding the Balfour Declaration, was that Palestine would become a national home for the Jewish people, the realization of a longtime dream. The hostility of the Arabs of the Middle East and North Africa was immediately aroused, and civil war erupted in the 1920's, in 1936, and in 1939. A British White Paper issued in 1939 closed Palestine to thousands of European refugees who wished to go there, and limited the Jews to settlement in an area representing a mere 6 percent of the total area west of the Jordan River. The Jews would thus become a permanent and ever-decreasing minority. Within ten years Palestine was to become an independent Arab state, under the terms of this White Paper.

The immediate result was the beginning of two underground movements against the British, made up of extremists. Zionist gangs became more and more active in acts of terrorism and guerrilla warfare. The largest group was the National Military Organization, the Irgun, with about a thousand members, which hoped to sabotage the British government and harass its officials; its main function was to destroy police stations and public buildings. A smaller but even more violent group was the Fighters for Freedom, the so-called Stern Gang of two hundred members, named for Abraham Stern, a Polish-born revolutionist of the Irgun, who was killed in Tel Aviv in 1942. These Sternists called for immediate establishment by force of a Jewish state; they attempted to assassinate the outgoing British high commissioner, Sir Harold MacMichael, who was shot from ambush and wounded outside Jerusalem on August 4, 1944. He was succeeded by Field Marshal Lord Gort, a World War II hero of Malta.

Meanwhile Lord MOYNE—Walter Edward Guinness of the famous brewer family—British Minister of State in the Middle East and Winston Churchill's chief minister outside London, was being blamed for the continued obstruction of the admission to Palestine of Jewish refugees from the Axis terror in Europe. One of the wealthiest men in Great Britain, Lord Moyne had previously served as Colonial Secretary and Deputy Minister of State. He bore the awesome responsibility of representing Great Britain throughout the Middle East, from Greece and the Balkan states south through the seething nations of the eastern Mediterranean to Egypt.

In waging its undeclared war against Great Britain, the Stern Gang vowed that Lord Moyne should become their victim. The assassins, two young Sternists, twenty-two-year-old Eliahu Bet Zouri and seventeen-year-old Eliahu Hakim, struck on November 6, 1944, in Cairo.

At 12:30 P.M. on that day, after a morning of work in his headquarters at the British embassy, Lord Moyne entered his official car with his secretary and aide. Arriving at Lord Moyne's suburban home, the driver, Lance Corporal Arthur Fuller, got out and hurried around to open the car door for the minister. The aide, Captain Arthur Hughes Onslow, got out and walked to the door. As he opened it, two figures vaulted over the fence and shrubbery to the back of the car. Brandishing revolvers, they immediately wrenched open the back door and fired three times at Lord Moyne. Almost simultaneously the captain was felled by three shots. Grappling with the assailants, Fuller was shot and killed instantly.

Inside the car Lord Moyne lay slumped in his seat. One bullet had lodged in his neck, another in his stomach, and the third, meant for his heart, had missed and gone through the dress of his secretary without touching her. She hurried to help the gasping driver, who died as she bent over him.

The two youths had meanwhile mounted their bicycles and were pedaling frantically, with Captain Hughes-Onslow bleeding from his wounds, in pursuit on foot. At that moment an Egyptian motorcycle policeman appeared and observed the scene in the courtyard and the two fleeing bicyclists. With an ear-splitting roar of his motor he set out after them, shouting, "Stop, murderers, stop!" As he gained distance on them, one of the boys turned and fired at the tires of the motorcycle but missed. The policeman fired at the boy, whose bicycle went out of control as he staggered in his seat and lost his grip on the wheel. Rider and bike crashed to the pavement. His companion made a wide circle to come back to his companion's rescue. The crowd which had witnessed the gun duel pounced on them, pummeling, kicking, ripping off their clothes. Within seconds the policeman had collared the two. One of the boys was bleeding from a wound in the chest. The other boy said simply, "We have nothing to say. We await the judgment of mankind," a statement typical of dedicated assassins.

Lord Moyne died that night after an emergency operation by King Farouk's personal physicians. The Sternists lost no time in admitting their responsibility. "Two of our brave Fighters for Freedom . . . successfully achieved their objective in their dangerous mission, and liquidated an important and vital member of the enemy forces," stated their official communiqué placed under doors and pasted on telegraph poles.

The trial of the assassins in January, 1945, attracted worldwide attention, with the boys making many political statements and justifications for their deed. They steadfastly refused to involve any other members of their group. They were finally condemned to death and hanged on March 22, 1945, unrepentant to the last, with Hebrew prayers on their lips.

The underground terrorism continued unabated and hundreds were eventually killed. But the principal victim was to be assassinated four years later.

When Swedish Count Folke BERNADOTTE was appointed United Nations mediator for Palestine, conditions in the Arab-Jewish confrontation had reached an impasse. The period 1939 to 1949 was a tragic decade. The violence of Jewish terrorism, of the Anglo-Jewish conflict and the Arab-

Jewish war kept the area in turmoil, largely due to the fact that the Arabs were unwilling to let the Jews have Palestine and the Zionists were determined to keep it at any cost. On the basis that the mandate had proved unworkable, Great Britain turned the problem over to the United Nations early in 1947. A Special Commission on Palestine suggested partition as a solution, and the General Assembly by majority vote approved this recommendation, which proved completely unacceptable to the Arabs. Following a short war, the Palestinian Jews on May 14, 1948, declared the independence of the state of Israel. In an endeavor to end the hostilities, the United Nations sent the Bernadotte mission to Palestine. The count arranged a truce and presented a partition plan which appeared to be a solution to the problem.

Previous to this appointment by the United Nations, Count Bernadotte, a nephew of King Gustav of Sweden, had attained an international reputation for humanitarian work, particularly in the International Red Cross.

Though mediation of disputes has long been an accepted method of settling disagreements between unions and management, its use on the international level was first begun by the League of Nations and continued by the United Nations in its consideration of the Palestine question. Mediation implies an effort by an outside party to assist the disputants in reaching a solution when a deadlock has occurred. Count Bernadotte was the first of a large number of U.N. representatives to undertake such a mission. Such mediators operate in ticklish, always emotional, international situations where infinite patience combined with tact and an open mind are essential.

Bernadotte had encountered a great deal of opposition

from the Jewish terrorist groups, particularly the Stern Gang, and the truce plan inflamed them because it appeared to favor the Arabs. Four days after the plan had been submitted and made public on September 18, 1948, Bernadotte went to Jerusalem to make a final inspection before leaving for his home in Sweden. He was accompanied by Colonel André SEROT of France, a United Nations observer, and Colonel Frank Begley, a United Nations security officer. Count Bernadotte was aware of the hatred he had aroused by his proposal, but he had traveled freely at all times in the confidence that his privileged position as a neutral and unarmed official representing the United Nations would not be defiled. Five other men, observers and guards, had been previously killed; two of these were deliberate assassinations.

Near the Hebrew University his car, a cream-colored Chrysler bearing the United Nations flag, was hit by a sniper's bullet. A few minutes later, in an Israeli-held former Arab residential district, the automobile was stopped at a roadblock. From a jeep stepped two men in Israeli army uniforms, carrying Sten machine guns. While the driver grappled with one of the men, the other looked into the car, recognized the count, shoved his gun through the window, and started shooting. The bullets went straight through the ribbons over Bernadotte's heart. Colonel Serot was hit seventeen times and killed instantly. Still breathing, Bernadotte was rushed to a nearby hospital, where he died on arrival.

The assassins were never apprehended, and though they were presumed to be members of the Stern Gang, the Israeli government failed to fix the blame with exactness.

The count may be said to have lost his life in vain, for

even though the new nation of Israel has flourished, the historic enmity and hatred between the Arabs and Israelis still continue, making the Middle East one of the continually troubled areas in the modern world.

chapter twelve

THE FAR EAST AND SOUTHERN ASIA

The term "Far East" generally includes the countries of East Asia—China, Japan, and Korea—and sometimes adjacent areas. Southeast Asia begins with the Philippines and extends to the south, including Vietnam, Burma, Thailand, Laos, Cambodia, and Indonesia; Ceylon is arbitrarily included for discussion in this area.

Almost all these countries remained uninfluenced by the West until the middle of the nineteenth century. Most were influenced by China until they became dominated by European colonial powers. The days of the vast colonial empires having ended, they are now independent. Political interest in them has been quickened with the tensions of modern times. The United States, in particular, has devoted attention to them as it has grown into the major world power. The containment of Communism, greatly feared because of the proximity and influence of Red China, has been a major element in American foreign policy toward Asia, and many of these countries are now inextricably involved in the future of the United States.

CEYLON

Nonpolitical assassinations are particularly tragic because personal grievances are involved, a life is taken needlessly, and a distinguished leader is lost to a nation which sorely needs him. The murder of sixty-year-old Ceylonese Prime Minister Solomon BANDARANAIKE in Colombo, Ceylon's capital, on September 25, 1959, was such an assassination.

After obtaining an excellent background of English education, Bandaranaike returned to serve his country, renouncing Christianity for Buddhism. He plunged into the movement which resulted in Ceylon's independence from Great Britain in 1948. Eight years later he became Prime Minister, and survived many internal upheavals, including a particularly divisive struggle between Hindus and Buddhists.

Far from acting out of political motives, Bandaranaike's killer resented the leader's efforts to further the practice of Western medicine in the Colombo hospital where he was employed. The Prime Minister stubbornly refused to worry about personal safety, and every morning he received visitors and petitioners in his home, attentively listening with patience to their problems. On this morning, after an interview with the American ambassador, a monk in saffron robes approached him on the veranda. While Bandaranaike bowed low in the Buddhist greeting, another man in monk's robe drew near and pulled out a pistol. As the Prime Minister cried out his wife's name, "Sirima! Sirima!" his assailant fired again and again. By the time a guard had brought the assassin down with a wound in the thigh, four bullets had pierced Bandaranaike's liver, spleen, and large intestine. He died the next morning, after a five-hour operation. Before his death he had called upon the Ceylonese to remain calm and to "show compassion" toward the assassin.

The monk who fired the fatal shots and his companion were both practitioners of Ayur-Vedic medicine, an ancient form of Eastern native medicine in which herbs, hot compresses, and body massage are major methods of treatment. They worked in the hospital where modern Western medicine and methods were being introduced. That very evening Bandaranaike was scheduled to review the recommendations of an expert on Ceylon's rival East-West medical practices. Several other Ayur-Vedic practitioners were also arrested, and in 1961 the assassin was found guilty and two others convicted of conspiracy; all three received sentences of death by hanging, which were carried out in 1962, nearly three years after the act.

Following two insecure interim governments, Mrs. Sirimavo Bandaranaike became Prime Minister, after elections in which she was the candidate of the party of her late husband. She was the first woman to become Prime Minister of a modern state.

JAPAN

Though a seemingly tranquil people, the Japanese have throughout their long history witnessed an almost unparalleled succession of political murders. As a *Life* reporter expressed it after the latest assassination in 1960, "The perilous practice of assassination runs like a blood-red thread through Japanese history, a relic of the not-so-distant feudal past when personal honor meant far more than governments or political principles."

The classic example of this attitude is found in the true story of the *Forty-Seven Ronin,* famous in Japanese drama and literature, in which assassins are glorified. The incident took place between 1701 and 1703. A minor feudal lord inflicted a sword wound on a more important warrior lord, who he considered had insulted him. In compliance with a code which called for the death of a disrespectful member of a lower order, the authorities ordered the unlucky man to commit suicide and ordered the confiscation of his lands. His *samurai,* or warrior followers, became *ronin,* which was the term for masterless samurai who had lost their normal place in society and agreed to take revenge for their master. After waiting for two years, these forty-seven *ronin* broke into the palace of their lord's old enemy and avenged themselves fully by decapitating him and several of his *samurai.* They were much admired for their self-sacrificing loyalty to their master and became national heroes, and the government, instead of ordering their executions permitted them to atone for their crime by the honorable death of *harakiri,* which is suicide by the painful method of cutting open one's abdomen. This they did, and today their simple graves stand side by side in a quiet little temple compound in Tokyo.

The story of the faithful *ronin* is still used as an example to twentieth-century nationalists who maintain that a loyal citizen can and should take the law into his own hands when his country's honor is at stake. The tradition was followed in 1860, when Prime Minister Ii NAOSUKE was assassinated by a group of Mito *samurai* while en route to the imperial palace in the middle of a raging snowstorm. Their reason was opposition to the government's foreign policy of opening the country to Western influences. Intermittent attacks on public figures opposed to Westernization were to continue for forty years.

In 1869 Minister of Military Affairs Omura MASUJIRO, a strong advocate of a national conscript army, was stabbed to death in Tokyo by an assassin who resented his introduction of European ideas and methods into the military organization of the country.

Premier Okubo TOSHIMICHI, murdered in 1878, had put through an advanced program of government reform aimed toward a strong centralized state. His killer justified the act by saying that Toshimichi "obstructed public discussion, suppressed popular rights, and exercised political powers of government as if they were his own private prerogatives, erred in the conduct of foreign relations, and caused a decline in national power and prestige"—certainly a detailed indictment. In 1885 Mori ARINORI, the first Minister of Education and previously the first Japanese minister to the United States, fell victim to a murderer's dagger. He had established a completely revised system of national education based on Western models which his killer, like many others, had violently opposed.

The most prominent Japanese statesman in the last two decades of the nineteenth century, Prince Ito HIROBUMI, four times Prime Minister, had contributed greatly to the modernization of Japan and had framed the new constitution. His assassination in 1909, however, was not due to any dissatisfaction of reactionaries in his homeland, but to the wrath of a Korean nationalist.

Since World War I, three Japanese Premiers have been assassinated, as well as numerous military figures. The assassins drew their inspiration from the historical *ronin*'s concept of "honorable violence." The first wave, which began in the 1920's, was a reaction against the influences of the new parliamentary government—elections had first been held in 1890—which were increasingly successful in the democratization of the country. Extremists and fanatics often brought an end to the rule of a party whose actions they opposed by this form of direct action, political assassination. These single, lawless acts served to dramatize dissatisfaction with new policies and were at first condoned; public opinion usually regarded the assassins leniently as well-meaning but misguided, and fully exonerated and even honored them. The most prominent victim during this decade was Premier Hara TAKASHI, who, as the first commoner to hold that office, represented the beginnings of true democracy in Japan, in 1921. The fanatic murderer stabbed him in protest against his efforts to improve the postwar international image of Japan by making it a major naval power and a member of the League of Nations.

Then, in the 1930's, came a wave of assassinations of high officials, some of the most notorious of them by army officers struggling to maintain their superiority and their declining positions of power. In 1930, Premier Osachi HAMAGUCHI, whose principal interest was in international disarmament, was murdered. He had accepted the limitations placed upon the growth of the Japanese Navy by the London Naval Reduction Treaty, and was nicknamed "Tiger" because he was one of the first high officials to assert civilian control over the military. While waiting in a Tokyo railway station, he was shot by a fanatical patriot and member of a nationalist society, but did not die until exactly a year later.

In the 1930's, young army-officer cliques frequently used the device of assassination to terrorize civilians who opposed their aggressive plans in China. In 1932 a group of young naval officers and army cadets murdered Premier Inukai TSUYOSHI, head of the majority Seiyukai Party, claiming that by their act they were attempting to free the emperor from "evil advisers." In 1935 General Nagata TETSURAN, one of the leaders of the Army Ministry, who had reorganized the army by stripping it of much of its former authority, was assassinated by Colonel Sabuto Aizawa, representing the young-officer faction. The army had been very powerful and would not give up when democracy began to develop. Aizawa's statement of motives was typical of the radical elements: he "professed to be acting on a heaven-sent impulse," but was tried and executed.

In the next year, on February 26, 1936, military assassins plotted unsuccessfully to kill Premier Okada Keisuke after the public had elected for parliamentary government liberal candidates who opposed control by the military. By this long-planned coup they hoped to seize the government in a major revolt. Several hundred soldiers led by lieutenants and captains took possession of the houses of parliament, the war office, the metropolitan police office, and one of the hotels. They murdered several high officials, among them Takahashi KOREKIGO, Minister of Finance; General WATANABE, military inspector-general; and Admiral Makoto SAITO, keeper of the Privy Seal and one of the closest advisers of the emperor. Several ministers received advanced warning and escaped death; others stayed in hiding, along with some military leaders, within a barbed-wire enclosure behind the moats of the imperial palace. A cousin who resembled the Premier closely was shot by mistake. Keisuke escaped through the ring of rebels surrounding his house by passing himself off as one of the pallbearers at his cousin's funeral. Three days later the army and navy forced the rebels to surrender. They were dealt with summarily: thirteen army officers and four civilians were executed after a secret and quick trial. Tokyo was placed under martial law, and a genuine attempt was made to restore discipline among the forces.

This major coup attempt resulted in official repression of all dissident groups during the next decade. Though underground movements thrived, there were no major political murders until the closing days of World War II. Postwar Japan has been constantly beset by riots and a number of attempted assassinations based on the old *samurai* urge to take the law into one's own hands. These protests represent the reaction of conservative ultranationalists against both the growing freedom and equality in Japanese society and the mass demonstrations of leftists and Communists. The youth of the country have been continuously active in mounting protest demonstrations against policies of recent governments, and the police have been unyielding and ferocious in dispersing such mobs.

That the political ferment and fanatical behavior still exist was demonstrated most recently in the public killing of Inejiro AsANUMA, chairman of Japan's leftist Socialist Party, on October 12, 1960. The meeting, attended by about three thousand, was to be a political debate between leaders of the various political parties in the coming election. The Liberal-Democratic government of Premier Nobusuke Kishi had fallen in the previous July after he had been stabbed by a rightist. Asanuma had been a foe of the security pact with the United States and had helped foment the leftist riots which forced the cancellation of President Eisenhower's visit to Japan in June.

Asanuma was speaking when heckling began, led by a clique of rightists. Then, while the audience watched, frozen in horror, a slim figure in black student's uniform burst onto the stage from the wings, a foot-long Samurai dagger in his hands. Before the guards could seize him, he plunged the glistening blade into the speaker's chest. Asanuma, a big man of 211 pounds, threw up his hands and groped feebly to ward off his attacker. Again the student plunged the dagger into his victim. Asanuma tottered, then fell in a heap on the stage, blood pouring from his wounds. By the time a police patrol car had rushed him to a nearby hospital, Japan's Socialist chief was dead.

The act was undoubtedly the most thoroughly witnessed murder in history, for the meeting was being televised nationally. With many cameras on hand, it was almost certainly also the most fully photographed. The killer was a seventeen-year-old university student, Otoya Yamaguchi, son of an army colonel. He had stolen the weapon from his father. An ultrarightest fanatic, he had been in trouble with the police for his political activities many times.

Violence as a way of political life in Japan continues. Assassinations and threats are common, not as a prelude to the seizure of power, but as a "service" rendered by dedicated individuals who use this traditional method of ridding the nation of its "enemies."

LAOS

Civil war among the neutralists, Communists, and non-Communists in Laos, long a French protectorate but a constitutional monarchy since 1949, has divided the country since 1954. The Communist Pathet Lao, supported by Red China and North Vietnam, occupies a third of the country and engages in a continuous power struggle, and successive coalition governments have repeatedly failed to survive and have given way to renewed fighting.

A victim of this struggle for control was neutralist Foreign Minister QUINIM Pholsena. On the evening of April 1, 1963, he and his wife arrived at the door of their home in the capital city of Vientiane, returning from a party at the King's palace. On guard was a unit of army soldiers, and as Quinim mounted the steps, one of the soldiers stepped forward and fired a blast from his submachine gun that killed the Foreign Minister immediately and seriously wounded his wife. The nineteen-year-old corporal submitted to arrest calmly. He was quoted as explaining his act by saying, "He [Quinim] wanted to overthrow the coalition government. Let the world decide who is the greatest patriot."

The accusation was unfortunately true. Bitterly anti-American and overtly pro-Communist, Quinim had done his best to torpedo any workable neutralist coalition. Previous to being appointed to his post by Prime Minister Souvanna Phouma, whose ward he had been during his teens, he had allied himself and his party with the Communists and their army in the revolt against Laos' pro-Western government. As the pro-Communist representative in the cabinet, he actually worked against his colleagues while pretending to cooperate.

Shortly after his murder, the Laotian government established an eight-man commission to investigate the slaying. If its report has ever been made public, no announcement has been made to the outside world.

Fighting between the Pathet Lao and neutralist forces intensified during 1963–66. Infiltration of the Vietcong through Laos, by way of the so-called Ho Chi Minh trail, into South Vietnam has caused difficulties for the American forces. Though the Pathet Lao occupied some of Laos' northern provinces with 25 percent of its population in 1968, the threat still continues.

REPUBLIC OF VIETNAM (SOUTH VIETNAM)

Vietnam was one of the three states comprising French Indochina, and after World War II Communists attempted to take it over. After an eight-year war, from 1946 to 1954, the French admitted defeat and evacuated the country, leaving the outcome in question. The country was then divided into two nations—the Republic of Vietnam (South Vietnam) in 1955 and the Democratic Republic of Vietnam (North Vietnam) in 1959 under Communist control. Since that time the Communists under President Ho Chi Minh have attempted to seize the republic in order to achieve the unification of the two parts of the country.

The first President of South Vietnam was Ngo Dinh DIEM, who was supported by the United States as a part of its program for the containment of Communism in southeast Asia. Guerrilla fighting has persisted since 1956, with the Communist Vietcong, aided by North Vietnam, opposing South Vietnam, aided by the United States. Ngo was reelected to a second term in 1961.

A serious internal political conflict arose in 1963 when Buddhist groups representing about a fifth of the population charged the South Vietnamese government with authoritarianism and brutality. This and other government delays in reforms paved the way for a violent military coup on November 1 and 2 which overthrew the Diem regime. The first act of the insurgents was to block off all roads to Saigon's airport and to seize most of the principal government buildings.

The rebels, assisted by artillery and planes, attacked the presidential palace where Diem and his brother Ngo Dinh NHU, chief of the secret police, were holding out with fifteen hundred soldiers. Subsequent accounts of their deaths varied considerably; to this day the official version states that their deaths were "accidental suicide." They were supposedly killed in an armored car when Nhu scuffled with an army captain over a gun. Scarcely anyone believed this explanation.

According to a likelier version, the brothers were shot by a nervous soldier against instructions from the leaders of the revolt who had promised them safe conduct out of the country. Eight of the generals had telephoned the President and, taking turns, had given him their promises that he would be protected. He hung up without replying. Just before the presidential palace was actually attacked on the first of November, Diem and Nhu fled, disguised in the garb of Roman Catholic priests, and spent the night secretly in the home of a Chinese businessman. An army vehicle waited; it had been sent by the generals to protect the two men from possible lynching. One report stated that Nhu refused to ride in the car and cursed the soldiers. The brothers struggled with a soldier over a pistol, and he shot them both in the back of their heads. Later, pictures showed them both, their faces bloodied and bruised, Nhu's hands tied behind his back. They were secretly buried.

The murders and coup had international repercussions. Diem's widow accused the United States of "intolerable interference" and complicity in her husband's death. In an American tour she continued making these charges. In South Vietnam several bloodless coups followed, and ten regimes have risen and fallen. The undeclared war has continued with ever-mounting fury, a war which has divided the United States and resulted in a decline in the popularity of former President Lyndon Johnson, one of the reasons for the Democratic defeat in the 1968 election.

In a country riddled with wartime corruption of all kinds, occasional lone public officials are notable for their moral standards, immunity from bribery, and dedication to their tasks. Their actions inevitably create enemies, both private and public, who have real or imagined grievances.

Dr. Le Minh TRI, South Vietnamese Minister of Education in the cabinet of Premier Tran Van Huong and Huong's teacher in grade school more than three decades before, was assassinated on January 6, 1969. He had replaced an official who had been dismissed from the post early in 1968 after charges of widespread cheating in the annual final examination for senior-high-school students.

Following his appointment, Dr. Tri dismissed several top employees and transferred others. His particular target for reform was the higher education system of the country, which he referred to as "a garbage can from which [he] intended to remove the lid." The universities had become sanctuaries for young people attempting to escape being drafted into the army, which by agreement with American officials was to be increased in number. Minister Tri questioned many exemptions and discovered that scholarships for overseas study were being awarded on the basis of favoritism rather than merit. He canceled a number of study grants that had been given during his predecessor's tenure. In testimony before the House of Representatives Tri said that he had received several letters and telephone calls threatening his life.

The assassin struck as Tri was riding to his office in downtown Saigon. As the car stopped for a red light, two grenades in a paper bag were tossed by a man riding on the back of a motorcycle as it drew alongside. The killer escaped as the car burst into flames and exploded. Dr. Tri and his bodyguard-driver, their bodies mutilated, were thrown to the pavement by the impact. The driver was killed instantly, and Tri died ten hours later. His stomach had been riddled by shrapnel, an eye was gone, a leg broken, and his head smashed.

Following the established pattern, the assassination was at first blamed upon militant Vietcong whose activities had terrorized the capital for many months. But authorities arrested as the prime suspect a marine sergeant who had in his possession the license number of Tri's car and a partial description of his daily routine.

More recently, in March, 1969, South Vietnam's Premier Tran Van Huong was the target of an unsuccessful assassination attempt. Four Vietnam soldiers in uniform made the attack while the premier was riding in a motorcade of four jeeps; a man wearing a Ranger's uniform and carrying a pistol rushed up and opened fire on a traffic policeman who was clearing the way for the convoy. A cyclo, one of Saigon's three-wheeled open taxis, suddenly drove to the middle of the street. As wild firing broke out, two of the jeeps pulled up alongside the premier's limousine; the convoy sped around the cyclo and the President escaped. The terrorists were captured, and the taxi was found to contain a mine and two pounds of dynamite. The combination failed to ignite. The principal attacker later confessed to being an agent in the pay of the Communists, though the opinion was widely held that the assassination attempt had been a plot hatched by foes of Huong inside the government.

chapter thirteen

LATIN AMERICA AND THE CARIBBEAN

Since the time when they achieved their independence, the main fact of life in the countries of this geographical area—which includes Central America (seven nations), South America (ten nations), and the three largest islands of the Caribbean region (Cuba, the Dominican Republic, and Haiti)—has been the military's participation in and control of their governments. The armed forces have continuously organized coups and ruling juntas, and dictators have dominated the political scene. More soldiers than civilians have become Presidents; even the civilians who have been candidates have usually been sponsored by the military.

Dictators thrive under such conditions. Some have worked for the good of their countrymen; others have been cruel and repressive, plundering the treasuries and establishing favorites in high positions.

Rebellions and revolutions have been of such regular occurrence as to be commonplace. Assassinations have most often been accomplished during such periods. For example, by 1898 Bolivia had survived more than sixty revolutions and six presidents had been assassinated; by 1952 the total revolutions had reached 179. Altogether, the twenty republics had suffered over one hundred successful revolutions before World War I. Since 1930, South America has been shaken by thirty-nine military coups, affecting all of the continent's principal countries except Uruguay.

Between 1954 and 1961 four military strong men were murdered—Remón Cantera of Panama (1955), Somoza of Nicaragua (1956), Castillo Armas of Guatemala (1957), and Trujillo of the Dominican Republic (1961). Many others have been driven into exile.

The pattern of military dictatorship and absolute power exists even today. Three out of every four of the continent's citizens today live under a dictatorship of one form or another. In twenty Latin American countries, 123 million people live under military dictatorships and twelve million under civilian dictatorships. These leaders live under the threat of assassination, and the murder record is far from closed.

DOMINICAN REPUBLIC

Since the division of the two parts of the island of Hispaniola in 1844, this nation, originally called Santo Domingo, has suffered innumerable dictators, frequent revolutions, constitutional difficulties, serious foreign interference, and the bondage of poverty. No modern nation in the Western Hemisphere has experienced more violence. Murder has been almost commonplace, turmoil continuous. Power struggles and repression of the island's citizens have been familiar, in spite of the frequent intervention of the United States, the latest during the 1964 civil war. Three Presidents in fifty years have been victims of assassination.

One of the most unscrupulous of early absolute dictators was Ulises HEUREAUX, a Negro who held total power from 1882 until 1899. His rule was characterized by cruel and greedy despotism, and the country became totally bankrupt because of his financial manipulations. Not unexpectedly, he was gunned down in 1899 in an uprising led by a group of conspirators among whom was Ramón CACERES, who became Vice-President. He was elected President in 1908, and found it necessary to suppress several revolts. He was murdered by political enemies in 1911; the group's leader was captured and killed, and an extended civil war followed.

One of the cruelest dictators of modern times, almost a model of the type, Rafael TRUJILLO MOLINA, was President of the Dominican Republic for four terms, 1930–38 and 1942–52. His years of power were marked by both good and bad acts. He was a master of both reform and repression. Taking over a wholly bankrupt, corrupt, and revolution-torn nation, he gave his people stable government, a sound currency, schools, and hospitals. But he also murdered and imprisoned thousands.

He had risen rapidly to the highest army rank, commander-in-chief, by 1927, when he was thirty-six years old. Ruthless power was the secret of his success. In the elections of 1930, the army's bayonets ensured his victory by 95 percent of the vote.

Soon, the Dominican Republic was not only ruled by Trujillo, it was his property. He amassed an estimated 800 million dollars during his thirty-year reign, becoming its largest landowner and cattle raiser. He attained absolute control over his poverty-stricken people. No Dominican dared to speak out against him for fear of being tortured; no newspaper criticized him. The secret police upheld his power; like thugs they annihilated any who opposed their chief by inference or action. Troublemakers were summarily dealt with; for instance, when sugar workers imported from neighboring Haiti caused dissension in rural districts in 1937, ten thousand were killed. Trujillo's excesses finally affronted all civilized nations, including the United States.

Such a monster invited the attention of dissident would-be assassins who suffered from his tyranny. Plot after plot was uncovered and the conspirators slain. He had practiced murder so conspicuously, often being patently involved in the assassinations of political figures and even friends who opposed him, that it was only a question of time before he himself would become the victim.

Trujillo's absolute power continued after he declined to be a candidate for a fifth term in 1952. Quite naturally, his brother Hector, a mulatto, was elected President in 1952 and reelected in 1957, but he resigned in 1960. The dictator continued to be the real power of the country, however, and his influence was unabated.

The long-expected and inevitable assassination came on May 30, 1961, when Trujillo was sixty-nine years old. On that evening he decided to visit one of his many mistresses at his farm fifteen miles from Ciudad Trujillo. With only his chauffeur in the front seat armed with a submachine gun, he sat in the back seat of the automobile with his personal tommy gun beside him. Both men had side arms as well.

As the car progressed down a lonely country road outside the capital, a black Chevrolet pulled up behind. From one of its windows, a submachine gun opened fire. Then the seven attackers in the automobile swung past the dictator's car and cut in ahead, forcing it to skid over the grass center into the opposite lane. Already bleeding from a wound, Trujillo ordered his chauffeur to leave the car and fight it out. Lurching out himself, the dictator leaned across the rear fender, shooting with his pistol until he was cut down with twenty-seven bullets. The chauffeur had meanwhile opened fire and wounded two attackers before he too fell with five serious wounds. The conspirators then kicked Trujillo again and again, stomped on his face, and tore one arm out of its socket, then dragged the body to their car and placed it in the trunk before they made their escape.

The chauffeur, however, was not dead and had seen the leader of the plot, whom he identified as General Juan Diaz. Five others were quickly rounded up. The murder had been planned for three months, and the conspirators had waited for the proper time to carry out their scheme; they had been alerted that Trujillo was on his way to the countryside. Diaz's main motive was apparently revenge, not revolution.

A favorite of Trujillo's brother Hector, he had fallen into disgrace when some of his relatives had been implicated the previous year in an assassination plot which was uncovered. Five of the conspirators were eventually executed.

Trujillo was buried in Paris. One of the world's most durable and despised modern dictators, he had died, as he lived, in an orgy of brutality and blood.

GUATEMALA

Like other Latin American nations, Guatemala has had its share of turmoil. Ever since its independence was gained in 1839, the country has suffered recurrent revolutions and dictatorial regimes. Government corruption and inefficiency and graft have been the order of the day. Only one President during this period was assassinated. José BARRIOS, who had been President for six years, was killed in 1898 after he had declared himself dictator.

The most startling contemporary event in Guatemala was the overthrow of Communism, which had made inroads on the government beginning with a revolution in 1944. Until 1954 Communist domination was complete, but finally an intended Communist invasion and government take-over was put down with the military removal of President Jacobo Arbenz. This was the first of such defeats in Latin America, and Guatemala has served as an example of resistance to all extremists, including Communists.

In a struggle for power in 1949, the candidate opposing Arbenz was General Francisco ARANA, chief of the armed forces, who promised a more benevolent dictatorship. But in July, 1949, at a roadblock established by a group of his enemies on a bridge near the capital, Guatemala City, a group of men pushing a stalled car stopped their activities, approached the automobile of Arana, and shot him point-blank in the chest and arm. His companions were showered with pistol, rifle, and machine gunfire; one aide was killed and three others seriously wounded.

Arana's death left Arbenz virtually unopposed. The results of the election gave Guatemala Communist domination for six years, until Arbenz was forced to resign after a revolution paid for and inspired by the United States Central Intelligence Agency.

One of the three military leaders in this revolution was Colonel Carlos CASTILLO ARMAS, who became President in 1954 after he had led an underground movement from neighboring Honduras against the Communists. After overcoming the Communists, he began to "shape a bright new day" for Guatemala. The help of the United States, both financial and political, enabled him to sponsor a five-year, much needed economic-development plan. His years as President were marked by several Communists plots, student demonstrations, and strikes. It was almost inevitable that these plots against his life would eventually be successful.

On the evening of July 26, 1957, a guard in the presidential palace snapped his heels together and slapped his Mauser rifle to present arms as Castillo and his wife passed by. Then the man stepped back, flipped off one set of the hall lights, raised his rifle to his shoulder, and fired point-blank. One bullet hit the President directly in the heart, killing him instantly. The guard fired another round into the body, then fled toward the palace gate, firing at and missing both a screaming maid and the colonel of the guard. As his comrades rushed upon him from all sides, he put the muzzle to his throat and fired the last bullet in his five-round clip upward through his own skull. He proved to be a Communist fanatic who had undoubtedly been planted by agents of Arbenz, then plotting in Uruguay for a return to power. From that day successive Guatemalan chiefs of state have made sincere efforts to continue the slain leader's dedication to democracy.

Extremist political elements in this uneasy Central American country, however, were responsible for the assassination of the United States ambassador, John G. MEIN, on August 28, 1968. He was the first foreign service officer of that rank to be assassinated in the long history of American diplomacy. Since 1960 Guatemala had been infested by the hemisphere's most rabid band of Castro-Cuban insurgents who blame the United States for years of "exploitation" by American business interests and for the success of the 1954 revolution. Since his appointment in 1965, Mein had been instrumental in promoting social reform through the American-sponsored Alliance for Progress and had witnessed Guatemala's first completely free presidential election. This government was vigorously opposed by right-wing terrorists who joined the leftists in an orgy of murder, kidnapping, bombing, and arson that reportedly claimed up to four thousand lives. Two military attachés of an American mission had been murdered and two enlisted men wounded earlier in the year. The ambassador was a vulnerable target for assassination.

The murder had apparently been carefully planned. As Mein traveled by car down the main street of the capital after an official luncheon, several youths in two small Japanese-made cars forced his Cadillac to the curb and opened the rear door to force Mein out. Leaping from his car, the ambassador made a dash for safety, but fell under a hail of pistol and machine gunfire and died instantly. At least nine bullets struck his body. The assailants made a successful escape, and a reward of ten thousand dollars was offered for their capture. President Mendez Montenegro imposed a thirty-day state of siege which was not lifted until November 26. Three members of the Castro-inspired underground Revolutionary Armed Forces were identified as the killers, but they were not apprehended. An official statement indicated that they were trying to kidnap the envoy and hold him as a hostage for one of their terrorists who had been arrested four days earlier.

MEXICO

After a long and continuous struggle for independence, terminating in 1824, the republic of Mexico was afflicted by foreign interference and domestic revolutions, and dictators followed one another in rapid succession. A period of comparative stability began with the presidency of dictator Porfirio Díaz in 1877, and the nation came to rank foremost among the countries of Latin America during his six terms. After he fled from Mexico in 1911, a twenty-year period of anarchy led the country into an abyss of hopelessness from which it finally emerged again as a leading Latin American nation.

The revolution, which lasted from 1910 to 1930 and which tore Mexico apart, was the first of the twentieth-century revolutionary movements, launched a year before the Chinese Revolution began and seven years before the Russians undertook to change their society by violent means. Beginning in 1910 with a political upheaval aimed at toppling a dictatorial regime and establishing a more democratic system of government, the Mexican movement evolved during the next decade into a full-blown social and economic revolution.

The bloody revolutionary years saw the assassinations of four larger-than-life characters: Francisco MADERO, victim of a meddling American ambassador; Venustiano CARRANZA, rival of Villa and architect of a new and much-needed constitution; the idealistic, unambitious outlaw Pancho VILLA, murdered five years after he had withdrawn from public life; and Álvaro OBREGÓN, shot to death by an artist who had just sketched his portrait.

These assassinations took place against a background of violence, guerrilla warfare, political and party power struggles—a period when any leader might be struck down and when plots and counterplots were the order of the day.

Porfirio Díaz was a candidate for reelection in 1910. Francisco Madero, a gentle man who believed in democratic principles and had confidence in the ability of people to govern themselves, felt the need for new and democratic leadership and decided to become a candidate. While he was campaigning vigorously throughout the country, he was arrested and falsely accused of inciting to rebellion and insulting the person of the President. Five thousand of his followers were also imprisoned. Díaz was, of course, elected by an overwhelming majority.

When Madero was released from prison on bail, he fled to find sanctuary in the United States. From San Antonio,

Texas, he issued a call for a revolt. There followed small local rebellions throughout Mexico, which the Díaz government had neither the will nor the power to suppress. Agreeing to turn the government over to his Minister of Foreign Affairs, with a cabinet named by the revolutionists, Díaz left the country.

Madero won 99 percent of the votes in a 1911 free election, but during the next two years his many enemies led small revolts. The army organized a coup in Mexico City, and the dictator's nephew, aided by mutinous troops, seized the presidential palace on February 9, 1913, and took charge. The President and Vice-President José María PINO SUÁREZ were imprisoned. After negotiations in which the two deposed leaders participated with the members of the diplomatic corps, they agreed to resign in return for a promise that they would be permitted to leave the country. United States Ambassador Henry L. Wilson was responsible for this decision. He was later linked specifically with the assassination plot and was recalled by President Woodrow Wilson.

On the evening of February 27, the two prisoners were removed from the presidential palace to the Federal penitentiary. Madero started for the official car, but was motioned to another sedan, which he entered. Pino Suárez was seated in a second automobile. Both were flanked by soldiers. At eleven o'clock they approached the penitentiary. The first car stopped near the entrance, with the second close behind it. The major in charge spoke briefly with the guard at the gate, and then ordered the driver to turn and proceed along the wall toward the rear. The cars stopped before a small rear door to the prison.

As the ex-President, obeying the officer's order, stepped

from the car, the major pulled a gun from the waistband of his trousers and shot him in the back of the head. Almost immediately, Pino Suárez was forced from the second car, and his body was pumped with shots until it no longer moved. The lights of the penitentiary went out.

The band of assassins then aimed their guns at the two automobiles and started shooting, shattering windows and headlights and puncturing the sides but not shooting at the motors or gasoline tanks. The driver of the second car was ordered to return to the garage and threatened with death if he ever talked about what they had seen. The next day he was taken to the presidential palace and made to sign a document which he was not allowed to read.

The two bodies were meanwhile tumbled into the rear seat of the first car. The legs of the Vice-President's body hung out the door and were broken in order to get them inside. The bodies were delivered to the front entrance. The driver of this car was also forced to sign the document.

This document, issued later, formed the official explanation for the murders. It stated that two groups of armed men had attempted to release the prisoners, and had twice attacked the escort. A thorough investigation would later clear up the specific circumstances. The bodies of the victims were not buried with public honors, but instead were dumped into shallow graves at the penitentiary, only being released to the families after a period of bargaining. The official version of the murders went unchallenged until the major involved, who had been advanced to the rank of general, was defeated in a battle two months later and fled to neighboring Guatemala. It was not until June, 1915, that a full confession of the true circumstances was obtained.

A little over a fortnight after the murder of Madero, his successor, President Victoriano Huerta was forced to resign. A month later Venustiano Carranza was accepted as provisional President. Francisco Villa was once Carranza's friend and had won several important battles but was now disenchanted and was rebelling in the north. Another Carranza enemy was Emiliano Zapata, leading a revolt in the south. The two united against Carranza.

The United States attempted to restore internal peace by recognizing Carranza as President, and even imposed an embargo on shipping arms to Villa and Zapata, thus strengthening Carranza's constitutional government. He was inaugurated in March, 1917. A new and model constitution was passed in 1917 which embodied most of the reforms for which the revolutionists had fought. A rare degree of peace existed for three years, even though local revolts continued. When the time came for a new election, Carranza's rival was Álvaro Obregón. The northern state of Sonora proclaimed its independence from the Federal government and called for the removal of Carranza.

The President decided to leave the capital for Veracruz with a small body of soldiers, a few close friends, and five million pesos in gold and silver from the Mexican treasury. He intended to remain there until after the election, and his security was guaranteed by the local commander, Guadalupe Sánchez. When Carranza's train reached the mountains, however, Sánchez attacked it. With a few followers Carranza fled northward on horseback, and at the boundary line of Puebla a local chieftain, General Herrero, promised to serve as guide. He conducted the group through a blinding downpour of rain to the tiny village of Tlaxcalantongo at the crest of a mountaintop. Early in the morning of May 21, 1920, Carranza went to sleep in an Indian hut while rain fell steadily on the roof.

At about 4 A.M., the silence exploded with gunfire. From the back of the hut came shouts of *"Viva Obregón!"* and *"Muerta Carranza!* (Death to Carranza!)." One of the first shots struck the President high on the left thigh, then more and more shots poured into the dwelling. The shooting stopped; no one could find the attackers in the pitch-black night, the rain, and the mud. In addition to the wound in the left thigh there were three chest and stomach wounds. Herrero's explanation was that Carranza had "committed suicide."

Obregón ordered an immediate investigation, which fixed the blame properly on the general and his followers. After a short prison term, Herrero was allowed to go free. Rumors persisted that Obregón had been involved in some way; nevertheless he became Mexican President in November, 1920.

General Francisco ("Pancho") VILLA, the outlaw rebel leader from the state of Chihuahua, was a controversial figure during his life and has continued to be since his assassination. To some, Villa was a hero, a kind of Robin Hood, a protector of the poor against oppressors; to others, he was no more than a bandit and vicious killer. In either or both roles he was a vivid character who exercised great power during the Mexican Revolution.

Born in 1877, he was a member of the peon class, and his name was probably Doreto Arango. He assumed the name Villa after he had murdered a man when eighteen and escaped to neighboring Durango, where he joined a band of notorious cattle and horse thieves. Scores of charges were made against him and his associates, but he was never caught, for he knew the mountains and trails intimately, a knowledge which subsequently helped him when, at the head of armed forces, he fought first the Federal army and afterward the troops of Carranza.

He soon struck out on his own, making a successful career of raiding the haciendas of the rich landowners. These raids brought him a popular notoriety, for time and again he eluded capture, making laughingstocks of the authorities.

His career as a political figure began with the Revolution of 1910. As a rebel chieftain, he championed the cause of Madero. He and his band of brigands blackmailed scores of merchants, rich property owners, and even entire villages, promising raids upon them if they did not pay, and subsequently distributing these gains to the peons. After the murder of Madero, Villa set out to fight the soldiers of Huerta. He was able to muster hundreds of men who were dissatisfied with the Huerta regime, and he soon controlled the entire state of Chihuahua as military governor. Whenever he captured a town, Villa executed all Federal soldiers found there. Even prominent officials were captured and shot by his orders; some of the victims were forced to pay over large sums of money before being disposed of.

His star dimmed momentarily when he was defeated by the forces of Obregón, who later became the President. Resentful of American intervention in the affairs of Mexico, in March, 1916, Villa conducted his famous raid on Columbus, New Mexico, leading 150 men and killing sixteen American citizens. A reward of ten thousand dollars was offered for Villa, dead or alive. General Pershing and his

U.S. cavalry force were sent to Mexico to capture him, but Villa successfully eluded them. Toward the end of the year he was able to defeat the Carranzista forces and to regain control of Chihuahua. He again embarked on an orgy of murder, raided military trains, and killed hundreds of Federal soldiers. By 1919, however, he was forced to retreat in order to escape capture by the Carranzistas, and fled to safety in the mountains with a mere handful of men.

Villa finally surrendered in 1920, and the government gave him a large estate, where he lived in great luxury on the considerable fortune he had amassed. He died however as he had lived—by violence. Though he did not know it, two previous attempts on his life had been abandoned. On the morning of July 20, 1923, he drove to a nearby town to obtain supplies for his hacienda. Five men were with him. On the main street, a vendor raised his hand in salute and called out, "Viva Villa!" After he had passed, the man took a bandanna from his pocket and, glancing toward the end of the street, mopped his face. This was a prearranged signal.

The door and two street-facing windows of a house were opened and four rifle barrels appeared in each window. As Villa's car approached the intersection and began to make the turn, the rifles roared, first four from the windows on the left, then the other four, then the first four again. The automobile swerved wildly and crashed head-on into a tree. The firing continued. The men ran out of the house, still firing, but now the bullets were from pistols.

Although he had received several immediate wounds, including two in the head, Villa had succeeded in pulling his pistol from its holster. He fired once, killing one of the attackers. The assassins continued their volleys; one of them later said that he had emptied his rifle twice and his pistol three times for a total of thirty-three shots. In the end, five of the men were dead. Villa's body bore thirteen wounds.

As he had hundreds of deadly enemies, relatives and friends of thousands of victims, it is no wonder that at last some of his foes organized the plot that ended his life. His assassins, whose names were well-known, had been paid three hundred pesos each for their work. Though their identity was common knowledge, they escaped justice. Remembering Villa's career as an outlaw, robber, and relentless killer, most people felt that he had received his just due, delayed as it was.

General Álvaro OBREGÓN rose from an obscure ranchero to become President of Mexico, to which office he was elected in 1920, succeeding Carranza. He had supported Madero in the Revolution, and had been active in crushing local rebellions. A persistent enemy of Villa, Obregón finally caused the rebel's defeat in a battle in which he lost an arm.

When he assumed the presidency, Mexico was at peace for the first time in many years, even though the condition was only temporary. He differed from many leaders in that he remained a simple and dedicated man even when he rose to power. He identified with the millions of peons and for that reason was able to rally them to his cause. His activities in land reform, labor organization, and education of the illiterate population were landmarks in modern Mexican history. Unlike many of his predecessors he was not anti-American; he realized that the *gringos,* in spite of their occasional meddling in Mexican internal politics, sought to support a stable government. For an all-too-brief period of development, Obregón was the outstanding figure in the country.

Local revolts continued to follow the established pattern, but the administration of Obregón, from 1920 to 1924, was marred by opposition to the Catholic Church, which had become involved in politics under Huerta. Anticlerical fury swept Mexico, and during Obregón's administration there were many outbreaks of violence—bombings, street fights, and desecration of churches. This unrest was to lead eventually to his death.

During the four years following his term as President, Obregón continued to believe that all parties could be conciliated. At times his optimism seemed justified, but the organized resistance of the Catholics increased, and they became more and more militant.

At the urging of his many friends and admirers, Obregón again became a candidate for the presidency. In the summer of 1928 he was reelected. He considered the settlement of the religious schism to be his number-one problem. During his campaign two bombs had been thrown at the automobile in which he was riding, but the assassination attempt was unsuccessful.

On July 17 Obregón was honored at a luncheon in the garden of a restaurant in Mexico City. A young artist, who was later found to have shadowed the President-elect for several days, moved throughout the room with his sketch pad making caricatures of various officials at the head table. He made a quick sketch of Obregón, the moved on to others. Then, from a few feet away, he made a more careful sketch. He showed his sketchbook to those nearest the guest of honor. Finally, with his left hand, he offered the book to Obregón, thrust his right hand into his jacket, pulled out a pistol and fired directly into the President-elect's face. He continued to fire until his victim collapsed, face forward, on the table. Obregón died shortly after in the same automobile in which he had escaped the bomb attempt on his life.

NICARAGUA

Like other Central American states, Nicaragua, the largest and least densely populated, has been torn by strife between dictator-Presidents and would-be dictators since obtaining its independence from Spain in 1821. Revolutions have been frequent, and the United States has several times felt it necessary to intervene to insure continued stable governments. States of siege have been common. After a long period of discontent, the United States sponsored the candidacy of Anastasio SOMOZA, who as commander-in-chief of the army had subdued rebel forces. Elected President in 1936, he was the nation's strong man for twenty years until his assassination in 1956. Long a friend of the United States, he almost singlehandedly brought his formerly turbulent country into an era of peace and prosperity, not, however, without making formidable enemies. As a no-nonsense dictator, he traveled throughout his country well guarded.

Death struck while he was attending a convention of the Nationalist Liberal Party in León on September 21, 1956. That afternoon the member-delegates had voted that he be their candidate in the coming elections, and he was understandably flattered and proud. Highly popular with the common people, he went that night to a worker's club and mingled freely with the shirt-sleeved members. At about eleven o'clock he was watching the other guests dancing when a man walked up to him, pulled out a revolver, and began shooting. A friend of Somoza jumped on the assailant's back, deflecting his aim. Even so, four bullets struck the President—one in his spine, partially paralyzing his right leg, another in his right shoulder, a third in his thigh, and a fourth in his arm. Before he fired his fifth shot, the body of the President's attacker was riddled by a deadly fusillade from presidential bodyguards.

When the news reached Washington, President Eisenhower dispatched several surgeons to Panama City, where the best-equipped hospital in Central America was located. Somoza was flown there and was operated upon immediately. During the four-hour operation the bullets in the thigh and imbedded in the spine were removed. But these efforts were in vain, and he died eight days later.

This murder is an almost perfect example of magnicide. The assassin, a salesman, could of course never reveal his motive; witnesses counted twenty bullet holes in his body. But investigation brought out that he had obsession for martyrdom. In a newspaper article written shortly before, he had stated, "Immortality is the aim of life and of glorious death." Acquaintances recalled that he complained constantly about Somoza. He had apparently acted on his own, for there was no sign of revolutionary activity. As a contemporary writer said, "His act was patently suicidal, and his motive may well have been an itch for self-glorification." Slaying a prominent figure would achieve this object.

Because of this delusion of an unbalanced mind, Nicaragua lost its finest hope for the future.

PANAMA

Called the crossroads of world trade because of the Panama Canal, Panama, a republic since 1903, has been plagued with continual internal turmoil caused by nationalists who have "harangued, attacked, argued, rioted, and more than once revolted" because of the presence of the Canal Zone and the American citizens there. Alternating waves of nationalism and Communism have swept the country periodically, and a swift succession of Presidents has been the result. The decade of the 1950's was one of crisis and chaos, with political instability, revolutionary outbursts, and bloody riots becoming common. Dictatorships have thrived.

One of the most benevolent dictators was strongman President José REMÓN CANTERA, who had been chief of police under President Arnulfo Arias in 1949–51. In 1953 he was elected President and was immensely popular for the next five years. He proved to be a good friend to the United States and was a bitter foe of Communism in addition to being a stabilizing influence in the Canal Zone. His assassination on January 2, 1955, was senseless and puzzling; it seemed to have been too carefully planned and executed to have been an act of private vengeance, and was certainly not intended to spark a revolution, for no disorders of any kind accompanied or followed it.

On that Sunday afternoon Remón and his party attended the races at the Juan Franco racetrack. After the crowd had left and dusk was rapidly falling, he lingered in the presidential enclosure chatting and enjoying cooling drinks. Two men in dark suits emerged from an automobile outside the stands with small submachine guns cradled in their hands. They crawled behind a hedge twenty feet from where the President sat. Moments later bursts of machine gunfire sprayed the box. Two men died instantly, and Remón slumped to the floor, blood darkening his white sports shirt; a bullet had penetrated his right side. From positions of safety in the darkness, the gunmen kept the President's bodyguards pinned down for several minutes, then made their getaway in the automobile. In spite of five massive blood transfusions, Remón died two hours later from the bullet which had pierced his aorta.

A concentrated dragnet of suspects was undertaken by his successor, Vice-President José Guizado; detectives from New York City, Cuba, Costa Rica, and Venezuela were called in for the investigation. The outcome proved to be a shocker. A fortnight later Ruén Miró, a prominent attorney, confessed the murder, implicating Guizado, who had promised him a cabinet post as a reward for the shooting, as well as the President's son and two business associates. The National Assembly impeached Guizado, ordered his arrest, and appointed a commission to probe the crime. The murder weapon was found in the home of Miró's father; it had been purchased from a student. After an immediate trial, the commission reported that Guizado was both a collaborator and instigator of the assassination and also an accessory after the fact. It recommended that the assembly indict the former President, and ordered the trials of thirteen other Panamanians involved in the killing.

The conflict with the United States over the Panama

Canal has erupted several times since the death of Remón. The dictatorships continue, and true democracy is still far in the future.

VENEZUELA

Chaotic politics have always plagued this oil-rich nation. Revolts and revolutions dot its history since the time of the Great Liberator, Bolívar. Democracy has been far from realization, and in contemporary times the Communists have fomented disturbances.

Lieut. Col. Carlos DELGADO CHALBAUD had been a moderate dictator since he became President after a bloodless coup in 1948. As leader of a three-man military junta, he had been largely responsible for the first free elections in Venezuela's history, and had followed a middle road in policy and social reform until his assassination on November 13, 1950.

The murder was of a peculiarly brutal kind. His car was ambushed as he was being driven from his home to the presidential palace in Caracas. He was slugged, then kidnapped and taken to a lonely part of the city where a group of twenty men beat him mercilessly and finally killed him by half a dozen bullets in the back. The band was headed by a rabid rightist general who was later captured and shot while attempting to escape. Eighteen of the attackers were later arrested and jailed. Since capital punishment is forbidden by Venezuelan law, they were not executed.

There was no attempt at revolution and no further violence. The leader of the plot was known as Venezuela's "eternal revolutionist"; a doctor called him a paranoiac who saw in Delgado Chalbaud an "obstacle in his path who was denying him his rights." Dictators are always susceptible to attacks by men with such delusions.

One of the recent Presidents, Rómulo Betancourt, in 1958 succeeded the six-year dictatorship of Marcos Pérez Jiménez, who had maintained his power by cruel repression of any and all opponents; Jiménez' "reign" was literally a police state, with lush graft for insiders, until he was ousted in a military coup. Betancourt's presidency was marked by a number of serious terrorist outbreaks, all Communist-inspired, yet he persisted in reforms to benefit his people.

In June, 1960, he narrowly escaped assassination when a bomb exploded near his automobile. Two of his aides were killed, and he was wounded. The would-be killers parked their car on the road Betancourt would take to attend an Armed Forces Day ceremony. They placed two suitcases, loaded with sixty pounds of dynamite and a radio receiver, in the trunk, and hooked this up to a detonating device which could be operated from some distance away. When the President's car passed, one of the plotters standing two hundred yards away pressed the button of the detonator and the car exploded. The automobile was hurled onto the center grass strip and burst into flames. The President and his Prime Minister managed to pull open the left rear door; the chauffeur and Betancourt's aide tumbled out of the front seat. Rushed to a hospital, Betancourt was treated for first-degree burns on his hands and face, but otherwise he was unhurt. His aide, whose face was completely smashed by flying shrapnel, died immediately. A bystander had also been killed on the spot.

The attack was finally traced to Dominican Republic

Dictator Rafael Trujillo, who hated Betancourt with passion. The Organization of American States heard the evidence and voted unanimously for a trial. Before it could be held, however, Trujillo was himself assassinated.

In Latin America, dictators as well as Presidents of good will still live in the constant danger that their lives will be snuffed out by assassins.

chapter fourteen

∧∧∧∧∧∧∧∧∧∧∧∧∧∧∧∧∧∧∧∧∧∧∧∧∧∧∧∧∧∧∧∧

KILLERS IN THE NEW AFRICA

Nowhere in the post-World War II world has there been more political upheaval than in the former Dark Continent. The dissolution of the extensive colonial possessions of European nations has been both abrupt and continuous as more and more of the demands of the local populations for independence have been realized.

Within the past decade 200 million people have secured their political, if not economic, freedom. Before 1945, Africa had four independent states—Egypt, Ethiopia, Liberia, and South Africa. After the war, the continent blossomed with new nations and new hopes. Algeria, Libya, Morocco, and Tunisia in the Muslim north became free. South of the Sahara Desert and in black tropical Africa, there appeared a bewildering array of nations, large and small, many of them with new names. By 1967, thirty-three new countries, former colonies of Belgium, France, Germany, Great Britain, Italy, Portugal, and Spain, were established. These transitions were accompanied by turmoil, strife, and even civil war. These early years have been marked by unbelievable violence; murders and the obliteration of whole tribes have been frequent, and may be expected to continue indefinitely.

Many of the emergent nations had been prepared for their new status by their former masters. Others became involved in internal power struggles which have threatened to tear them apart. A digest of major problems suggests the web of complications that entangles new Africa.

ALGERIA

France had held and occupied Algeria as a province since the mid-1800's. However, the French made no attempt to understand the Muslims, who constituted the majority of the country. Instead, they reaped economic benefits and tried to minimize the internal discontent. After World War II, the rising nationalism came to a head. Demands for a constitution, for French citizenship, and for an Algerian flag remained unanswered. A violent revolt in 1945 was ruthlessly suppressed. The seeds of revolution had been planted. Algerian nationalism passed from peaceful petition to bitterness which brought on war. November 1, 1954, marked the beginning of a rebellion which was to last for seven long, miserable years, at the cost of tens of thousands of lives.

Ahmed Ben Bella led a conspiracy of frightful violence, and finally General Charles de Gaulle arranged a settlement which led to self-government. Independence was declared in July, 1962, and Ben Bella, the sole candidate, became the first President in the fall of 1963. During the referendum shortly after the new state had been established, two bombs aimed at him were exploded while he was addressing a large crowd in Algiers in September, and one hundred were hurt, many seriously. Assassination rumors were officially denied.

The internal strife continued, however, and opposition to the government was intense. An assassin shot Foreign Minister Mohammed KHEMISTI on April 11, 1963. The murderer was described as a counterrevolutionary. Khemisti lingered in a coma for three weeks until his death. The killer was summarily executed.

Another unsuccessful attempt was made on President Ben Bella's life in June, 1964, when a bomb exploded with accompanying machine gunfire near his home in Algiers. The intended killer was sentenced to a life term in prison, but escaped the next year and was never tracked down. Ben Bella was deposed in a surprise bloodless coup in mid-1965. His enemies later sought him out in France, kidnapping but not harming him.

Though Algeria has become relatively calm, the prospects for more violence are ever-present.

BURUNDI

Under German control until taken over by Belgium after World War I, Ruanda-Urundi became a trusteeship under the United Nations. The territory is inhabited by two tribes, the Watutsi and the Bahutu, who have long conducted an undeclared war. In 1960 the country was divided and one part, Rwanda, became a republic in 1961. The other, Burundi, continued as a constitutional monarchy. Crown Prince and Premier Louis RWANGASORE, successor to the throne, was shot and killed on October 13, 1961, in a plot engineered by opponents of the independence which had been voted on the month before. Five participants were executed, one received a life prison term, and several others were jailed for terms ranging from seven months to ten years.

The blood feud soon emerged into open civil war between the two tribes in Burundi, each attempting to obtain sole government power. Villages went up in flames; crops and cattle were destroyed. In four days alone early in 1964, eighteen hundred persons were killed. Thousands were ruthlessly butchered. The entire nation was affected. Tiny Burundi had been the biggest base for Red Chinese subversion in the African continent, and a moderate Premier, thirty-year-old Pierre NGENDANDUMWE, a Bahutu, was appointed with the priority function of checking Peking's rising influence, since the Communists were encouraging the internal struggle and disunity. He sought fruitlessly to mediate the differences and bring about peace. The Watutsis became his implacable enemies.

On January 15, 1965, as he left a hospital in the capital, Bujumbura, after visiting his wife and new baby, he was riddled with bullets and died instantly. The assassin was a Watutsi refugee from Rwanda, employed as a typist in the United States embassy. Among others, he implicated five prominent government officials, including an ex-Premier who was Ngendandumwe's predecessor, an ex-cabinet minister, and a chief justice.

Rumors abounded. Because the slayer worked in the American embassy, the murder was characterized as an "imperialist plot by the United States," and led to a break in diplomatic relations. Another rumor circulated and widely believed was that since the Premier was investigating Red Chinese support for Congolese rebels along Burundi's borders, the killer must have been a Communist Chinese agent.

The official investigation by the new Premier brought seven persons to trial. The President absolved both the United States and Communist China of involvement, calling it a coincidence that the confessed assassin was friendly to the Chinese and also worked in the embassy. In all, twenty pro-Chinese members of the government and twenty-three Watutsi tribesmen were arrested, and Burundi eventually severed diplomatic relations with Red China.

Another Premier, Leopold Biha, was seriously wounded later in 1965. Burundi continues to be torn apart by the tribal enmity, and no solution can be expected in the immediate future.

DEMOCRATIC REPUBLIC OF THE CONGO

The confusion and turmoil which accompanied the transition of the many colonies in Africa into independent nations was nowhere more fierce and destructive than in this former Belgian territory. The complicated webs of internal sectionalism and external intervention by foreign powers finally led to the dispatch of a United Nations military force in 1960 to prevent a civil war.

The story of this unrest is one of primitive violence and murder, complicated by many factors. During its years as the Belgian Congo, the territory was ruthlessly exploited by its masters. This colony received its independence more suddenly than any others. Where other colonial powers had prepared for the transition to independence for years, even decades, the Belgians without warning announced the Congo's independence in 1960. In the first general elections the National Congolese Party placed Patrice LUMUMBA in the post of Premier.

The most powerful legacy of Belgium was the Union Minière of Haute-Katanga, which owned not only the highly productive copper mines but also the railroads, the air service, factories, and banks—practically everything modern in the Katanga Province near the Rhodesian border. Before independence, the Union paid about 45 percent of the Congo's annual revenues and 60 percent of Katanga's. Of all African colonial states, the Belgian Congo thus suffered the most from paternalism. Strict color discrimination against the black Africans was observed also; whatever was done for them was designed to develop "good workers" for exploiting the mineral riches of the country, and they had no voice in the government. The granting of independence almost immediately destroyed the semblance of unity in the new republic. The Europeans were set upon by the natives, and Belgian troops remained to maintain order. Congolese troops mutinied against the Belgian citizens, causing the majority to leave the country.

The province of Katanga seceded under the leadership of Moise Tshombe, who became its President. The lines were drawn for a civil war.

Tshombe strengthened his position by refusing to permit either President Joseph Kasavubu or Premier Lumumba to enter his province or United Nations troops to be stationed there. Katanga fighters and white mercenaries maintained their hold, and United Nations Secretary-General Dag Hammarskjöld was killed in an airplane crash while en route to negotiate a cease-fire.

Meanwhile the chief of staff of the Congolese Army suspended both Kasavubu and Lumumba from their duties, announcing that he would cooperate with the United Nations. By the end of the year Lumumba, realizing the dangerous position in which he found himself in planning a military invasion of Katanga, attempted to leave Leopoldville, the capital, but was arrested and imprisoned on a warrant signed by President Kasavubu. Later he was flown to Elisabethville, the capital of Katanga. Two of his closest friends, Youth Minister Maurice Mpolo and Senate Vice-President Joseph Okito, went with him. On arrival they were hauled off the plane and savagely beaten by Katanganese soldiers, then allegedly driven to jail with their hands bound behind their backs with ropes. The rest was a mystery which was not revealed by Kasavubu until a month later, with further details announced by a United Nations Commission of Investigation seven months afterward.

The Katanganese Interior Minister made the first announcement: "If people accuse us of killing Lumumba, I will reply, 'Prove it.'" The official version was that the three had escaped from their farmhouse prison in a stolen car. The car ran out of gasoline and was found overturned in a ditch forty-five miles away. Three days later, fleeing on foot, they were "massacred" by the inhabitants of a small village.

"The villagers may have acted somewhat precipitously, though excusably," the statement continued, and they would be paid the eight thousand dollars bounty that had been posted for Lumumba's head. The Interior Minister would not name the village because of "eventual reprisals," nor would he say where the three bodies were buried for fear of later "pilgrimages to the scene."

The United Nations Commission report stated that the three victims had been killed by direct order of Katanga President Tshombe immediately on their arrival on January 17. As the three disembarked from the plane, the Interior Minister approached Lumumba and, after a few remarks, took a bayonet from the rifle of one of the soldiers accompanying him and plunged it into Lumumba's chest. As the Premier lay wounded, a Belgian mercenary serving in the Katanga Army administered the fatal bayonet thrusts. The other two were simultaneously bayoneted. The disposition of the three bodies has never been revealed.

The United Nations troops remained in the Congo until 1964, and, amid occasional eruptions of local violence, the nation is still struggling for a permanent peace.

SOUTH AFRICA

While political turmoil and tragedy have torn apart many of the newer nations of Africa, human tragedy has been unfolding in the most prosperous of African countries. South Africa has brought upon itself worldwide condemnation and appears to the outside world to be determinedly set upon a course of self-destruction.

The racial policy of white supremacy became the official government policy of apartheid in 1948, and led to the country's withdrawal from the British Commonwealth and the establishment of a republic in 1961. The word "apartheid" in Afrikaans means "separateness." In application it means racial segregation—that is, the policy of segregation and political and economic discrimination against non-European groups in the country. In 1967 the population was made up of almost thirteen million Bantus (blacks), three and a half million whites, almost two million coloreds (mixed), and a half a million Asiatics. The policy of white supremacy, officially called "separate development," denies to the Bantus, the population majority, any share in the central government. The Nationalist Party, representing the Afrikaners, the white South Africans of Dutch descent who number 60 percent of the total whites, took an even firmer stand on segregation when Dr. Hendrik F. VERWOERD became Prime Minister in 1958. Persecution and imprisonment have been the lot of those who have overtly opposed the government policy.

The Bantus have struggled to set up their own internal governments in certain areas, and local self-government has occasionally become a reality, but the wrongs of apartheid have continued. As the symbol of this detestable and inhuman system, Verwoerd met with persistent opposition. In 1960, native Africans were required by law to carry identification passes, and in a protest at Sharpeville police fired on a crowd, killing sixty-seven protesting blacks and wounding 183. Three weeks after this massacre, the Prime Minister himself was felled with bullets, fired into his head at point-blank range by a would-be assassin. He had just finished a speech at a park in Johannesburg. His words, characteris-

KILLERS IN THE NEW AFRICA

tically, had been strident and militant. "We shall not be killed," he told his audience. "We shall fight for our existence." He returned to his box and sat down. Moments later, a fifty-two-year-old farmer named David Pratt entered the box and fired twice with a pistol, hitting Verwoerd in the cheek and ear. Verwoerd slumped to the floor as guards grappled with the assailant. In court, Pratt explained his act: "I think I was shooting at all apartheid, rather than at Dr. Verwoerd." Declared mentally unfit to stand trial, Pratt hanged himself in a mental institution a year later. After six weeks in a hospital, the Prime Minister was released with two small scars as souvenirs and discovered that the support of his Afrikaner followers had been increased. He stated, "I know that I have been spared to complete my life's work." Because of his survival, he was looked upon by his followers as a God-protected leader.

During the 1960's Verwoerd succeeded in legislating additional restrictive laws, but spent millions of dollars on housing and education to improve the lot of the disenfranchised blacks. He proved successful in overcoming much of the worldwide criticism, even within the United Nations, but never veered from the basic policy of apartheid.

His death by violence appeared inevitable, and the day of his doom finally arrived in Cape Town on September 6, 1966.

On that afternoon, when postluncheon bells summoned the members of Parliament to their seats, Verwoerd took his place on the Prime Minister's bench. He was to deliver a speech detailing the latest triumphs in his unrelenting campaign to continue the racist policies of the government. A few moments later, a middle-aged man wearing the Parliament's green-and-black livery shoved through the incoming throng and headed toward him. As the Prime Minister, expecting a message, glanced up, a knife flashed out, up, and down. Without a word, Verwoerd sprawled dead across his desk with four vicious stab wounds in the heart and throat. Five doctors, four of them members of Parliament, tried desperately to revive him with heart stimulants and mouth-to-mouth resuscitation, to no avail.

The murderer, forty-five-year-old Dimitrio Tsafendas, was wrestled to the ground and suffered a smashed nose and broken jaw in the scuffle. He proved to be a mulatto who was passing as white. His strange explanation for the act was that the Prime Minister was "doing too much for the coloreds and not enough for the poor whites." At his trial later in the year he was declared insane and ordered to be detained in prison indefinitely. He had been a mental patient during preceding thirty years in five countries, including the United States, and had escaped from at least two institutions.

The assassination failed to change the basic government policy. Verwoerd's successor, Balthaser Vorster, has maintained the shame of his country.

TOGO

This new republic, set up in 1960, was formerly a part of the German colony of Togoland which was divided between France and Great Britain in the Treaty of Versailles after World War I. This geographical partition proved to be unwise, creating bitterness among the citizens. A strong nationalist movement began in French Togoland (Togo) after British Togoland joined Ghana in 1956. Fortunately President Sylvanus OLYMPIO was skillful in advancing the status of the new country. He was pro-West, and his intelligence and statesmanship were much admired. His ambition was to transform Togo into the "model democratic state of Africa."

The principal difficulty was the opposition of Ghana's President Nkrumah, who wanted to incorporate Togo into his country. The instigators of the plot to assassinate Olympio, however, were Togolese who had served in the French army before independence, but had not been taken into Olympio's army when they were demobilized. The life of a head of state is generally threatened by a large opposition group, but Olympio's assassin was one among the comparative few affected by this army policy. The President had refused to expand the four-hundred-man army to make room for these men. When they became suddenly unemployed, they decided on vengeance.

On the morning of January 13, 1963, Olympio, while walking alone on the streets of Lomé, the capital, was killed in a burst of gunfire. His body was found huddled just three feet outside the unlocked gate of the United States embassy building. Apparently he had been murdered while attempting to seek political asylum there. The killer, an ex-sergeant, readily confessed the deed, saying that when a group of his fellow soldiers approached the President to detain him so that they could argue their cause, he resisted and attempted to flee. Only then was he shot down.

More turmoil followed, and an army group seized the government, arrested the cabinet ministers, and recalled one of Olympio's enemies, who had been exiled, to form a cabinet. Before his death, Olympio had initiated a vast program for the betterment of his country, which was well on the way to becoming the model republic he had hoped for, so his loss to Togo was indeed a tragic one.

chapter fifteen

GUNS IN THE UNITED STATES

The record of assassinations of heads of state forms an ugly piece of Americana, particularly since the United States is a democracy. Political murders have been frequent in monarchies and dictatorships, but the fact that four of the thirty-six American presidents have been murdered and that five attempts have been made is completely without parallel among nations. The occurrence of assassination within five years in the 1960's—the two Kennedys and Martin Luther King—has resulted in much soul searching by the American people and by psychiatrists, sociologists, and other authorities on human behavior. They attribute it to the climate of violence in which we live, and, as *Time* states it, "impatience with political process and a resort to violence."

The unsuccessful attempts which have been made on the lives of American public officials have been the acts of unstable individuals who have formed grievances against their targets because of an assumed injustice or wrong, to an individual or to a cause. The successful murders have almost without exception been accomplished by individuals with the same turn of mind.

The first attempt on the life of a United States chief executive occurred in 1835. The target was Andrew Jackson, the sixth President, and the setting was the portico of the Capitol, where as a member of the funeral procession of Representative Warren R. Davis of South Carolina, the President was walking with the Secretary of the Treasury. On this Friday, January 30, at about noon, a house painter, Richard Lawrence, stepped from behind a pillar at the east portico and, taking from his pockets two brass percussion-cap pistols, deliberately aimed at Jackson. The caps exploded without firing, and the President was saved. At the trial four months later (the prosecutor was Francis Scott Key, the author of "The Star-Spangled Banner"), the motive of Lawrence was revealed as imaginary grievances against Jackson. In two White House interviews the President had refused to give him the money he felt was his due, and in Lawrence's disordered mind this refusal was coupled with financial ruin and death, which he illogically—it occurred long before Jackson entered the White House—blamed on the President. The jury brought in the verdict of "not guilty, he having been under the influence of insanity at the time he committed the act." Lawrence was committed to jails and mental hospitals for the rest of his twenty-six years; the modern diagnosis in his case would be schizophrenia of the paranoid type.

The next attempt was made upon the life of the sixteenth President, Abraham Lincoln. This was the famous 1861 Baltimore plot. When Lincoln arrived at Philadelphia en route to Washington and the inauguration, Allan Pinkerton informed him that his operatives had uncovered an assassination plot hatched there. Baltimore was extremely pro-Southern, and eight men had been selected to kill the President-elect as he passed through the city. This was confirmed by information from Washington. Boarding a train to Baltimore rather than to Harrisburg as had been planned, Lincoln disguised himself with a beaver hat and an old overcoat and began the journey late on the night of Feburuary 25, 1861, in the last sleeping car. On arrival in Baltimore at about 3:30 the next morning, his car was detached, pulled by horses through the darkened streets to another station, and attached to a train on another line. He arrived safely. The complete story of this plot has never been told. The next violence against a President was Lincoln's assassination in 1865.

Lincoln's murder was followed by two others—Garfield in 1881 and McKinley in 1901. The next attempt was made on the life of former President Theodore Roosevelt, who had become the twenty-sixth President after the assassination of William McKinley and had been reelected in 1904. Following his terms of office, he continued to take an active part in politics, and was in Milwaukee, Wisconsin, on a campaign tour in October of 1912. As he left his hotel and entered the automobile which was to take him to the Milwaukee auditorium where he was scheduled to make a speech, a figure emerged from the darkness, raised a revolver, held it above the heads of nearby spectators, and pulled the trigger. Roosevelt was standing and waving to the crowd when the single bullet struck him in the right breast, where it bored inward and upward about four inches, fracturing the fourth rib. The shot had been fired at a distance of about six feet, and the bullet would have torn through his lung had it not first struck the breast pocket of his coat, in which he carried the folded fifty-page manuscript of the speech and his spectacle case. The bullet had to pass through not only the case but a hundred pages of paper and therefore lost much of its force before penetrating the flesh. Had it not been for this, Roosevelt undoubtedly would have been killed. The assailant was tackled and disarmed.

Undaunted by this act, courageous T.R. insisted on delivering his speech before receiving medical attention. He spoke fifty minutes with the bullet in his chest, then went to a hospital. He carried the lead bullet in his chest until his death seven years later. The would-be assassin was John M. Schrank, a New Yorker, who had trailed his victim through eight states waiting for the propitious moment. He had been told in a dream that a third-termer must be regarded as a traitor and should be forcibly removed. "I am willing to die for my country," he had written. "God has called me to be his instrument, so help me God." A sanity commission of five alienists examined him. Their report that he was insane led to his commitment to a Wisconsin mental hospital where he remained for thirty-one years until his death in 1943.

More than two decades later, another Roosevelt, Franklin

Delano, the thirty-second President, narrowly escaped death in Miami, Florida. On February 15, 1933, with his inauguration only two and a half weeks away, Roosevelt and his official party were entering the center of the Bayfront Park Ampitheatre, where he was to make a speech, when Giuseppe Zangara, a bricklayer from New Jersey, fired five continuous shots at clear range from a nearby seat. Five persons were hit, but the President-elect was not. One of the five was Chicago's mayor, Anton CERMAK, who died on March 6, two days after Roosevelt had taken the oath of office.

Seventeen years later, in 1950, President Harry Truman, Roosevelt's successor, in his second term of office, escaped unhurt from the attack of two Puerto Rican nationalists who attempted to shoot their way into Blair House, his temporary residence while the White House across the street was undergoing repairs. At about two o'clock on the afternoon of November 1 Oscar Collazo and Griselio Torresola from New York set their plan in action. Collazo approached from the east, Torresola from the west, with the intention of meeting at the Blair House steps and shooting their way inside. A White House policeman was near the entrance at the top of the steps. Collazo drew his pistol, pointed it straight at him, and pulled the trigger, but the weapon misfired. The guard was not hit until he started down the steps; then Collazo's bullet grazed his right leg. (This was the only one of nine shots, fired by Collazo during the incident, which hit its mark.) As the policeman drew his gun to return the fire, Collazo started up the steps. As he did so, the guard and Secret Service agent in the east sentry booth began firing at him. Collazo was shot in the chest and fell to the sidewalk.

Meanwhile Torresola walked up to the west booth, took aim with his Luger automatic pistol, and shot the guard three times, then turned to aim three shots at another White House guard who came on the run from a side door. Then he shot the guard Collazo had wounded, before he himself fell mortally wounded from the bullets of the west booth guard who later died. Two men had been fatally shot and three others wounded. President Truman, napping in his front room on the second floor, was awakened and witnessed a part of the action.

At the hospital where he was treated for his chest wound, Collazo told a nurse the reason for the attempt: He was a Puerto Rican nationalist and wanted his country to be free. Collazo was indicted on four counts. His defense in his 1951 trial was that he and his companion had wished only to create a "demonstration" to advance the cause of Puerto Rican independence, but that Torresola had gone berserk and killed the officer. Before being sentenced to execution by electrocution, he stated that what he did was "for the cause of the liberty of my country." President Truman later commuted the sentence to life imprisonment.

In 1954, three years after the Blair House shooting, a group of four Puerto Rican nationalists, three men and a woman, fired pistols at random from the spectator's gallery of the House of Representatives shouting for Puerto Rican independence. Five Congressmen were wounded but recovered. The attackers were given prison sentences.

PRESIDENTS

Full accounts of the four assassinations of United States chief executives—Lincoln, Garfield, McKinley, and Kennedy—are readily available in histories, biographies, periodicals, and newspapers. Only the basic outlines of the acts themselves are included here, with special attention to the motives of the murderers and their warped personalities. Only in the case of Lincoln's assassination was there a conspiracy; the other men acted on their own and for reasons they considered valid.

The murder of President Abraham LINCOLN in Washington on April 14, 1865, was not only the first successful assassination attempt but was also shocking in the complexity of its repercussions. Occurring as it did five days after the end of the long and tragic Civil War, it had an accordingly greater impact on the reunited country than any of the three assassinations which followed over the years.

General Ulysses S. Grant was to have accompanied the presidential party to the performance of *Our American Cousin* at Ford's Theatre, but his plans were changed during the afternoon. President and Mrs. Lincoln sat with their party of three in a box to the right of the stage. Just before the end of the play at a little past ten o'clock, John Wilkes Booth, an actor, entered the box, closed and fastened the door behind him, and with a derringer pistol in one hand and a dagger in the other, rested the former on the back of the chair occupied by Lincoln and shot him. The ball entered Lincoln's ear, passed through his brain, and lodged near one of his eyes. The attacker was seized by Major Henry Rathbone, one of the party. Booth dropped his pistol, struck Rathbone on the arm with the dagger, tore away from his grasp, and rushed to the front of the box with the gleaming weapon in his hand. Shouting, *"Sic semper tyrannis!* (So may it always be with tyrants!),*"* the motto on the state seal of Virginia, he leaped to the stage. He was booted and spurred for a night ride, and one of his spurs caught in a flag and he fell. Rising, he turned to the audience and shouted, "The South is avenged!" Then he escaped by a back door where a horse awaited him.

The President died without regaining consciousness the next morning, April 15. Booth was pursued and overtaken twelve days later in a barn in Virginia. He refused to surrender, so the barn was set afire and the assassin shot by a sergeant. The full-scale plot was not long in being revealed. Lincoln had received many threats against his life, and he kept them in an envelope marked "assassinations"; this once contained eighty threatening letters. A month before he had dreamed of being killed. Though bodyguards had accompanied him to the theater, Booth had been able to elude them by careful and detailed planning.

A part of the comprehensive plot called for the simultaneous murders of Secretary of State William Seward and Vice-President Andrew Johnson, first in line as Lincoln's successor. While Booth was murdering the President, another of the nine conspirators, Lewis Paine, visited the home of Secretary Seward, second in the line of succession. His pretext for entering was that he was a messenger from the doctor and carried some medicine for the Secretary, who was in bed with a broken jaw. On the second-floor landing he was met by Seward's son Frederick, who insisted his father could not be disturbed. Paine smashed his head with a revolver and entered the bedroom, where he drew his knife, first slashing the male nurse, then Seward himself. The knife ripped open the Secretary's right cheek and sliced both sides of his neck. Before he ran out of the house shouting, "Murder! Murder!" Paine had stabbed three other attendants. Vice-President Johnson escaped only because the conspirator who had been assigned to kill him lost his nerve and passed the evening in a tavern.

The conspirators were finally rounded up; one, John Surratt, was taken prisoner in Alexandria, Egypt. After the trial in the spring, four were hanged and four were imprisoned in the Dry Tortugas. Three of the prisoners were pardoned by President Johnson in 1869; the other had died of yellow fever. Tragedy was to strike twice again before effective protection was to be offered to American Presidents.

Booth left abundant documentation which, supplemented by the trial testimony of his fellow-conspirators, forms an excellent study of the anatomy of assassination. He was a thorough paranoid with a history of alcoholism, and his life was filled with psychotic episodes. A diary entry written when he was being sought read, "I can never repent it, though we hated to kill. Our country owed all her troubles to him [Lincoln], and God simply made me the instrument of His punishment. . . . This was not a wrong, unless God deem it so, and it's with Him to damn or bless me."

The threat which hangs over all Presidents next became a reality to James GARFIELD, the twentieth President. On July 2, 1881, shortly after nine o'clock in the morning, he arrived at the Washington railroad station to board a train for Long Branch, New Jersey, where he was to spend his vacation at his summer home. He was accompanied by Secretary of State James Blaine. As they passed through the ladies' waiting room, a man came up behind Garfield, pulled out his revolver, and fired. The President straightened up and threw his head back. "My God, what is this?" he exclaimed as he staggered. The shot had struck Garfield in the back and smashed into his abdomen, and he fell on his knees. A second bullet missed its mark but passed through the sleeve of his coat. The attacker calmly put the pistol in his pocket and surrendered himself to the police.

At the White House doctors found that the wound was serious. The bullet had fractured two ribs, gone through the backbone, and cut a large artery before becoming imbedded in the pancreas. For six weeks his condition worsened, and because of the heat he was taken to Long Branch, where he died on September 19.

The killer, Charles J. Guiteau, had planned his attack for two months, believing "that if the President was out of the way everything would go better." Guiteau had a long record of failure; he had been involved in many unsuccessful schemes and possessed delusions of grandeur. He had offered himself as a Republican campaign speaker in New York City and had been rejected after only one speech. After the inauguration he went to Washington to find employment in the new administration as a reward for his efforts. He first pestered the two Senators from New York, but was turned away every time he approached them. Having decided that the consulate in Paris was the proper assignment for him, he made advances to Secretary Blaine again, with no results or encouragement. He decided to lay siege to the White House and bombarded Garfield with notes. Receiving no replies and being continually turned away by exasperated secretaries, Guiteau decided that he had been wrong in backing the President and offering his services; furthermore, he reasoned, Garfield was the cause of all the trouble within the Republican Party. After purchasing a revolver he began to wait for the President to expose himself alone. Without knowing it, Garfield had had several narrow escapes before that fateful morning.

The trial began in mid-November and lasted nearly two months. Always talkative, Guiteau claimed he was not a "disappointed office seeker" as he had been characterized, but a man "chosen by supreme powers to execute President Garfield and thus save the nation." The trial was the first in the United States to involve the question of sanity; his defense counsel maintained that he was insane, but Guiteau said he was not. The question was never settled, for he received a death sentence and was hanged in June, 1882. Psychologists have analyzed his motivation as "magnicide," the desire to kill someone prominent. He wanted above all to be important, and he had aimed high. He had expected to be praised and applauded for his "contribution" to the successful election. When this did not happen, "God instructed him" to become a presidential assassin. When he heard the jury decision of sane and guilty, he shouted, "God will avenge this outrage!" As he went to the scaffold, he recited an original poem based on "John Brown's Body." His last words were, "Glory, glory, glory!"

A somewhat different type of assassin shot the next victim, President William MCKINLEY, on September 6, 1901. That morning he made a speech at Niagara Falls and was scheduled to be present at an afternoon public reception to be held at the Temple of Music of the Pan American Exposition then being held in Buffalo. His advisers worried about his safety, but he overrode their objections, telling them, "Why should anyone want to harm me?" He was a popular President.

Since the public was to be admitted to shake hands with their chief executive, a few uniformed police, detectives, and soldiers were assigned to the presidential party. As the doors opened at four o'clock, McKinley took his place, and those waiting began to be admitted. Among them was Leon Czolgosz. To conceal his pistol Czolgosz, who had been in line for an hour, had wrapped it in a handkerchief in his right hand, as though it were a bandage. As he arrived face to face with the President, the latter, seeing the bandaged hand, pulled back his own outstretched right hand and was about to extend his left for the handshake.

Czolgosz immediately fired twice through the handkerchief, at such close range that the powder stained the President's vest. McKinley hesitated, then fell backward. One bullet had struck him in the breastbone but went no farther, the other ripped into his stomach and lodged in the pancreas. As soldiers and detectives knocked him down and beat him severely, Czolgosz muttered, "I done my duty." McKinley, still conscious, said quietly, "Easy with him."

The President was rushed to a hospital for a ninety-minute emergency operation, then to the home of the exposition chairman. The pancreas wound was the same kind of injury Garfield had suffered twenty years before. McKinley lost ground rapidly and died of gangrene on September 14.

In his jail cell, Czolgosz wrote out his confession: "I killed him because I done my duty. I don't believe one man should have so much ceremony [attention] and another man should have none." He admitted that he was an anarchist, but a conspiracy was never uncovered. His trial, held four days after McKinley's funeral, lasted only eight and a half hours, and the jury found him guilty after deliberating only thirty-four minutes. An alienist had testified that he was legally sane though undoubtedly mentally ill. He had been a loner and a wanderer, never able to hold a job. He admitted that he decided to kill the President four days before he did so. He had listened to McKinley addressing an audience of an estimated fifty thousand at the exposition the day before, and told the court, "I saw a great many there saluting him, bowing to him, and honoring him. It was just not right."

And so, because no one paid any homage to him, Czolgosz snuffed out a life. Just before his electrocution the last of October, he made a final statement: "I killed the President because he was the enemy of the good people, the good working people. I am not sorry for my crime."

The murder of John F. KENNEDY, thirty-fifth and youngest (forty-six) of United States Presidents, in Dallas, Texas, on November 22, 1963, was, in the words of the Warren Commission, "a cruel and shocking act of violence directed against a man, a family, a nation, and against all mankind. A young and vigorous leader whose years of public and private life stretched before him was the victim of the fourth presidential assassination in the history of a country dedicated to the concepts of reasoned argument and peaceful political change." The shock of the sudden tragedy numbed a people who had all but forgotten the bloody past and who had been lulled into the belief that "it can't happen here."

This was one of the first of several assassinations to be televised to a nationwide audience, from the murder act to the burial, and the nation reeled under the shock and grief.

The facts are familiar to every American. On that day Kennedy was to speak before a gathering of business and political leaders at a 12:30 luncheon at the Dallas Trade Mart. The presidential party began a motorcade through downtown Dallas at about noon. The lead car bore President and Mrs. Kennedy in the rear seat, and Texas Governor John B. Connally, Jr., and his wife occupied the jump seats. Two Secret Service agents, one of whom was the driver, were in front. Directly behind the presidential car was an open follow-up car with eight Secret Service agents, who were to follow the usual procedures of scanning the crowds, roofs and windows of buildings, overpasses, and crossings for signs of possible trouble. Behind this car was the Vice-Presidential automobile carrying Mr. and Mrs. Johnson and Texas Senator Ralph Yarborough. A Secret Service follow-up car was next, and then other automobiles and several buses for additional officials, and press representatives. Mr. Kennedy rode without the bubbletop, a plastic shield which had been devised as a protection only against inclement weather; it was later bulletproofed.

The motorcade moved slowly, and as it approached the entrance to the Stemmons Freeway, past Dealey Plaza, it was moving at a speed of about eleven miles per hour. The front of the Texas School Book Depository, a seven-story, orange-brick warehouse and office building, was to the right.

Seconds later shots resounded in rapid succession. The President's hands moved to his neck, and he slumped forward. A bullet had entered the base of the back of his neck slightly to the right of the spine; it traveled downward and passed out from the front of the neck. Almost at the same time Governor Connally was hit by a bullet which entered the right side of his back below his armpit and traveled

GUNS IN THE UNITED STATES   **183**

downward to his left thigh. Another bullet then struck President Kennedy in the back of his head, causing a massive and fatal wound. He fell to the left into his wife's lap. Two agents in the follow-up car rushed to cover the two couples, and the car gained speed and raced to Parkland Memorial Hospital, four miles away. By 1 P.M. John Kennedy was pronounced dead.

Eyewitnesses reported that they had seen a rifle being fired from the southeast corner window on the sixth floor of the Depository. Within two minutes a motorcycle policeman had run up the stairs to the second floor. There he encountered a man whom he passed quickly; the man's name was Lee Harvey Oswald. Oswald hurried home to pick up the pistol with which he killed a Dallas patrolman, J. D. Tippit, when stopped by him for questioning. Oswald was apprehended in a moving picture theater. Oswald was held under tight security until Sunday. On that morning, in full view of a national television audience, he was murdered by Jack Ruby, the operator of a striptease joint in Dallas, who attacked Oswald as he was being moved from the city to the county jail. Ruby died before his second trial.

Investigation into his childhood proved that Oswald had been characterized then as "potentially dangerous," a youth with a schizoid personality, full of hate and confused in his thinking. Unstable and rootless, he had wandered many years as a loner. He was an admirer of Castro and a student of Communism, and had spent eight months in the Soviet Union before returning to the United States in June, 1962. He continued in his Communist leanings. In January, 1963, he ordered a pistol from a Los Angeles firm; this was the weapon with which he killed Officer Tippit. Later he ordered by mail the rifle which was used in the assassination.

A presidential commission under the chairmanship of Chief Justice Earl Warren was appointed a week after the tragedy to report the full truth concerning the assassination. The 726-page "Summary and Conclusions," based on the full sixteen-volume report, was released on September 27, 1964. All the facts concerning the tragedy and Oswald's activities and background were covered in detail. Five hundred and fifty-two witnesses testified. Scores of conclusions and findings on the assassination itself were listed. The report also included recommendations regarding Secret Service protection.

The statement, "The Commission has found no evidence that either Lee Harvey Oswald or Jack Ruby was a part of any conspiracy, domestic or foreign, to assassinate President Kennedy" caused a furore. Oswald's motives, it stated, could not be definitely determined, except that he possessed an urge to find a place in history, had a capacity for violence, and possessed an antagonism toward the United States evidenced by his defection to the Soviet Union and his frustrated efforts to go to Cuba.

At least eighteen books have been written in support of a conspiracy theory, by people who do not agree with the Warren Commission report. The Harris poll has revealed that in 1968 two thirds of Americans were still convinced that President Kennedy was the victim of a conspiracy. To lay to rest the speculation that more than one gunman was involved, a confidential report was issued by the United States Attorney General in January, 1969, stating that a panel of four physicians agreed with the commission that the two bullets were fired from the same weapon and that there was no crossfire. This was based on the evidence of the autopsy which had not previously been made public.

Whatever the truth, another president—"a dashing young Irishman blessed with every gift of the gods—youth and money and brains, grace and looks"—had fallen victim to an assassin.

No protection was given United States Presidents during the first hundred years of our history. Even after Lincoln's murder, little was done to safeguard the lives of chief executives. Only after the assassinations of Garfield and McKinley was action taken. By 1902, the statistics were appalling. In thirty-seven years, three Presidents had been assassinated, an average of one every twelve years. This situation was unparalleled in European countries, where attempts on the lives of European rulers and heads of state, although frequent, had usually been unsuccessful. Presidents of a democracy were assumed to be safe as a matter of course; they had been chosen by the people. To have a chief executive surrounded by guards at all times was intolerable, suggesting as it did the pomp of European royalty.

But with McKinley's death the country was roused to action. The Secret Service, founded in 1865, had been concerned mainly with counterfeiters. During the presidency of Theodore Roosevelt, in 1907, the full-time responsibility for protecting the chief executive was assigned to the Secret Service. In 1913 this was broadened to include the President-elect, and in 1917 the members of the President's family. Not until 1951 was protection given the Vice-President.

Living former Presidents and the widows and children of former Presidents are currently supplied with full-time Secret Service agents.

These guards have never worn uniforms, but they are constantly present, accompanying their charges in all public appearances. Part of the duties of the Secret Service involves the examination of all threats received by the White House. Though this activity has been given little publicity, hundreds of such crank letters are received, and all are thoroughly investiagated.

In spite of exceptional precautions, John F. Kennedy was shot down. The report of the Warren Commission devoted a great deal of space to suggested overhauling of the protection activities of the Secret Service; its techniques have been subsequently improved and its resources enlarged. After the assassination of Senator Robert Kennedy, all presidential candidates were allotted agents, and during the 1968 campaign these agents were always in evidence. At the inauguration of Richard Nixon on January 20, 1969, eighteen hundred army and National Guard troops were in Washington to supplement the protection of the Secret Service. Special agents concealed from sight and armed with automatic weapons equipped with wide-angle devices scanned the throngs along the route between the White House and the Capitol. Helicopters with Secret Service agents hovered over the cars carrying Richard Nixon and Lyndon Johnson. The Nixon automobile, a closed limousine, was flanked by eight agents, four on each side. The new President, his family, and his cabinet members reviewed the inaugural parade from behind bulletproof glass.

During the campaign and after, such figures as Senator

Everett Dirksen and Senator Edward Kennedy were reported to have received death threats. Leading government officials have now lost all freedom of movement; they are virtually the prisoners of their protectors.

The Federal law provides that anyone who mails or utters a threat to assassinate or physically harm the President is liable to maximum penalties of one thousand dollars and five years in jail. After the murder of President Kennedy, there was a 100 percent annual increase in the number of known assassination plots against the chief executive. There were more arrests for plotting or threatening to murder Lyndon Johnson than for all other Presidents combined. Only twelve arrests per year were made for plotting to kill President Truman. No more than nineteen such arrests occurred during the eight years that Dwight Eisenhower was President, and an average of only thirty-five arrests for threatened assassination were made each year while Kennedy was President.

But in 1964 there were more than a hundred arrests for threatening to kill President Johnson. In 1965, the arrests increased to two hundred; in 1966, there were more than 410 such arrests and in 1967 at least 428! In addition, in 1968, 353 "unwelcome visitors" to the White House were detained for psychiatric examination. Even the monitored telephone calls were frequently abusive and threatening; of 12,740 in that category, 1,139 investigated by the Secret Service revealed the callers as potential assassins. Most of the subsequent trials and prison sentences under the law were not publicized, in the belief that other potential assassins might seek to make themselves martyrs.

There is little reason to view the future with complacency. The climate of violence in which the United States currently exists, in spite of increased security measures and precautions, may lead to even more threats and assassination attempts. President Richard Nixon began receiving threats after his inauguration, and in May a man carrying brass knuckles and a can of MACE was taken into custody at the gates of the White House; in his car, police found a loaded automatic pistol, a loaded shotgun, another can of MACE, a tear-gas grenade, and a gas mask. In the same month, the writer of a threatening letter was arrested and given a jail sentence.

SENATORS

One of the most audacious and flamboyant figures in twentieth-century American politics was Huey LONG. During the 1930's his name was as well-known as that of President Franklin Roosevelt. Though he received no education beyond high school, he became the self-proclaimed "Kingfish" of Louisiana, the poor man's friend. He was, for a short time, the king of all he surveyed. After his election as governor in 1928, he placed favorites in all state government jobs, and impeachment proceedings against him failed.

When he was elected to the United States Senate in 1930, he bypassed the formality of an election and installed a friend as governor to replace him. During the postdepression years of 1934 and 1935 he made himself a presidential possibility with his "Share-the-Wealth" program which assured his followers of a guaranteed annual unearned income. His slogan was "every man a king"; his appeal was anti-Semitic, anti-Negro, and anti-Roosevelt, and his popularity was constant. As governor he had demanded and received a kickback of a percentage of the salaries of all state employees, and this was said to have continued when he became Senator. He was second to none as a rabble-rouser. Corruption and bribery were the order of the day.

Dr. Carl Weiss, the obscure dentist who assassinated Long in the state capitol building in Baton Rouge on September 8, 1935, had viewed with concern and alarm the tenacious hold Long held on the state. As the Senator left his office with other officials on that evening, the young man, wearing a white linen suit and holding a straw hat in his hand, emerged from behind a column, raised a hidden pistol at arm's length, and fired once, striking Long in the right side. As Weiss was about to fire a second time, bodyguards grappled with him and in the struggle shot him two times. A number of other guards then ran up and pumped his fallen body full of bullets.

Still completely conscious and not yet aware of the seriousness of his wound, Long was taken to a nearby hospital and given a massive blood transfusion before being operated on. His wound was of the same nature as those inflicted on Presidents Garfield and McKinley. He died the next day.

The motives of Weiss were never exactly pinpointed. He may have been the executioner chosen by a group of plotters. He may have held a grudge because his father-in-law, a judge, had been deprived of his long-held post. He may have been a dedicated man who murdered Long for the common good, destroying a dictatorship through the death of the autocrat who stood at its head. The truth will probably never be known.

Few political assassinations have shocked the people of the United States more than the murder of New York Senator Robert F. KENNEDY in Los Angeles, California, on June

5, 1968. Many witnessed the tragedy on television, and in the following days millions of citizens shared a common feeling of stunned grief, intensified by the memories of his brother's death.

A few minutes before his murder he had been declared the winner of the Democratic presidential nomination in the crucial state of California. His tireless campaign had been followed closely, and at a time when the country was torn with violence and crime, his seemed to many to be the voice of reason.

The details of Senator Kennedy's murder are still fresh in the minds of Americans, many of whom viewed the act on television almost as if they were present. At about 12:15 A.M. on June 5, Kennedy left the ballroom of the Ambassador Hotel after the victory announcement. He was passing through a kitchen area on a shortcut to a news conference. Lurking in the crowded corridor, a young man named Sirhan Bishara Sirhan swiftly pumped eight shots of a pistol at point-blank range in rapid succession at the Senator's head. Three bullets struck Mr. Kennedy, and five bystanders in the crowd were wounded. Kennedy fell to the floor, blood gushing from his head. His friends seized the assailant and disarmed him.

Of the bullets, one had grazed Kennedy's forehead. Another had lodged in his neck. The third, entering behind the right ear, had smashed its way into his head and damaged three parts of his brain. These wounds proved fatal, and the Senator failed to survive an operation. He died the next day.

Sirhan was a twenty-four-year-old Jordanian who had come to the United States eleven years before. His early life had been spent in Jerusalem, and his hatred of Israel was both bitter and intense. His determination to kill the Senator had become fixed when Kennedy had spoken out strongly for sending United States arms to Israel and repeatedly called for an end to Jordanian raids against Israel. As he was being dragged away from the pantry area, Sirhan shouted, "I can explain. I did it to save my country." In his pockets were found a schedule of Kennedy's June speaking engagements and an article describing the Senator as a "hawk" in the Middle East situation. Authorities later found, in a notebook Sirhan had kept, an entry made after Kennedy vocalized his support for Israel during a television debate with his opponent, Senator Eugene McCarthy, on June 1: "Kennedy must be assassinated before June 5, 1968." In later entries the two words "Kill Kennedy" were repeated time and time again. After a lengthy trial in the spring of 1969, Sirhan was found guilty of murder and given a death sentence.

There were two immediate results of the assassination. For the first time in American history all candidates for the presidential and vice-presidential nominations were to be given continuous Secret Service protection; and during the remainder of the year local, state, and Federal gun laws were revised and tightened.

A GOVERNOR

The battles of political party competition occur on all levels. Deadly and implacable enemies are made, but seldom do such differences erupt into political assassination. However, at least once a life was lost: the time, January 30, 1900; the place, Frankfort, the capital of Kentucky; the victim, William GOEBEL.

As a Democratic state senator since 1887, Goebel encountered bitter Republican political opposition. He even shot to death one of his rivals in 1895, but his power was so great that a grand jury refused to indict him. His enemies increased when he introduced reform legislation aimed at taxation and railroads.

In 1899 he was a candidate for the Democratic nomination for governor and secured it in the Louisville convention by a series of shrewd political maneuvers which greatly increased his unpopularity and divided his party. The result was a highly charged and exciting campaign, resulting in the election of his Republican opponent, William Taylor, by a very small majority. After Taylor was inaugurated, Goebel charged fraud and contested the election before the legislature, which had Democratic majorities in both branches.

While the proceedings were in progress, Goebel left his hotel en route to the state house to testify. As he reached the gate, a shot was fired from a window of the three-story building. He fell to the sidewalk, and several other shots were fired but went wild. Governor Taylor immediately called out the state militia, and for several days Frankfort was an armed camp.

The next day the legislature met and declared Goebel governor. The oath of office was administered at his hospital bed. On February 3 he died.

The fatal bullet which had passed through Goebel's body had been found imbedded in a tree. Based on the position of the governor and the angle at which the bullet had passed through his body, investigators decided that it had been fired from the window of the office of Secretary of State Caleb Powers who was captured in Lexington. The case of

Powers finally ended in the United States Supreme Court, which ousted Taylor as governor and charged Powers as an accessory to the assassination. Two hired assassins had fired the shots. Powers was found guilty in a new trial. The man who had supplied the gun and the killer who had fired it were sentenced to life imprisonment, but they were pardoned by Governor Augustus Willson in 1908.

MAYORS

Like other elected officials, city mayors invariably acquire enemies, not only on the basis of their policies and administrative actions but also for their actions in the dispensing of favors and the political patronage which the office involves. Though civil service is intended to control the qualifications and quality of appointees on many levels, a good many positions are filled by the mayor himself, with or without the advice and recommendation of the political machine in power. As a result, a disgruntled citizen may develop a persecution complex and may even try to kill the man he holds responsible for his plight.

A discharged municipal employee attempted to assassinate New York's Mayor William Gaynor in August, 1910. Seven months after he had assumed office, Gaynor planned a European vacation. While he was talking with reporters and friends on the deck of the liner *Kaiser Wilhelm,* a man stepped from the crowd and pressed a gun at the back of the mayor's neck, sending a bullet crashing into his throat.

The would-be assassin was James J. Gallagher, an employee of the Docks Department who had been discharged for neglect of duty. In seeking reinstatement he had been sent from office to office, but no one would listen to his complaint. The mayor had been unavailable. Gallagher finally convinced himself that Gaynor was the main cause of his troubles. "He took away my bread and butter," he said after his arrest.

The bullet lodged in the mayor's throat and remained near his larynx the rest of his life, causing a harsh, rasping cough and reducing his voice to a whisper. He died three years later in the deck chair of the steamer on which he was taking his postponed trip.

A notable assassination was that of Chicago's Mayor Carter HARRISON, who was elected five times. Though he was a wealthy aristocrat, his continued power lay in his sympathy with the common people; he was in both words and acts their champion. Under his first four administrations, from 1879 to 1885, the city rose from the ashes of the great fire of 1871 to become a booming metropolis. He was reelected in April, 1893, and became the official host to the World's Columbian Exposition, one of the most spectacular exhibitions ever to be held in the United States.

Three days before its closing, on October 28, Mayor Harrison delivered an afternoon speech celebrating American Cities Day with many United States and Canadian mayors in the audience. In those days elected officials made themselves available to citizens both in their offices and homes. Appointments were not necessary. After dinner at his home that evening, Harrison was summoned to the front parlor to meet a visitor, a lawyer named Prendergast. Without warning, Prendergast fired three shots into the mayor's body. Harrison fell to the floor and never regained consciousness. He died within fifteen minutes. The slayer went immediately to the local police station and surrendered.

Prendergast had sought an appointment as city corporation counsel so that he could effect a change in surface transportation. Specifically he wanted to have elevated tracks built for the cable cars, which had been involved in many fatal pedestrian accidents, and "to put a stop to the slaughter of the people." He thought he was performing a service to the citizens by the assassination.

In the subsequent trial the defense entered a plea of "insanity and irresponsibility" because, as a child, Prendergast had hurt his head in a fall. The jury found him guilty of first-degree murder, and he was sentenced to death.

In the assassination of Chicago's Mayor Anton CERMAK in Miami, Florida, on February 15, 1933, the intended victim of assassin Giuseppe Zangara was President-elect Franklin D. Roosevelt. Like all Chicago mayors, Cermak counted on the new administration to repay the huge Democratic vote in the city, which as usual had given the State of Illinois to Roosevelt. At the suggestion of James Farley, Cermak went to Miami to see the incoming President and remind him of the Federal patronage he expected his city to receive.

When Roosevelt arrived in Bayfront Park, Cermak was in the front seat of the reviewing stand. The President-elect rode by in the official car. Seeing Cermak, he beckoned to him, but the mayor did not approach him at that moment. Roosevelt gave a short speech from the automobile. When he had finished, Cermak along with other dignitaries approached him. They exchanged a few remarks. Roosevelt's auto was about to start when shots rang out. Cermak was hit, as well as four others.

The crowd attempted to seize Zangara, but police rescued

him. Roosevelt's car shot ahead as the bloodied Cermak shouted, "The President! Get him away!" Still standing, the mayor was helped by two companions to the presidential car, which had halted. Roosevelt and Cermak rode to the hospital together. The bullet had pierced Cermak's right lung and become lodged in a vertebra. For nearly three weeks Cermak lingered between life and death. He finally died on March 6.

A great deal of credence was given to the theory that Cermak was the intended victim and that the assassin had been hired by Chicago gangsters, but such rumors were proved false by Zangara's statements. He was very voluble and produced a variety of reasons for attempting to kill Roosevelt. He admitted making the trip to Miami for that purpose, and clippings describing the President's plans were in his pocket, together with several describing the assassination of McKinley. "I'm sorry I didn't kill him," Zangara said. "I want to kill all Presidents, all officers. I did not hate him personally; I hate all Presidents, no matter where they come from, just like I hate all officers and everybody who's rich. . . . I have done my own thinking and I reached this decision by myself."

Zangara was sentenced to eighty years in prison before Cermak died.. After his victim's death, Zangara was tried again, charged with having murdered the Chicago mayor in a premeditated attempt to assassinate President Roosevelt. He was declared legally sane, though a definite paranoiac. He was electrocuted thirty-three days after the crime. Zangara apparently enjoyed the attention paid to him, and even while the guards were arranging the foot plates on the chair and placing the cowl over his head he shouted, "Lousy capitalists!" His last words were "Go ahead. Push the button."

A NEGRO CIVIL RIGHTS LEADER

Leaders who are dedicated to a nonpolitical cause incur an enmity of a particular type. Rev. Dr. Martin Luther KING, Jr., was such a leader, a man devoted to the wider cause of human understanding as well as to the advancement of Negro rights. His bias-inspired detractors hotly resented the successes he achieved for his race.

King was not a man who encouraged violence. Like Gandhi he developed a technique of civil disobedience of passive resistance. Minister of the Dexter Avenue Baptist Church in Montgomery, Alabama, Dr. King first used this method of nonviolent Negro protest in that city in 1955–56 with a successful boycott of the local segregated bus system. This form of protest spread throughout the South and the North. The movement was a means of demanding the rights of Negroes as citizens—the rights given them in the Federal Civil Rights Act of 1957 and later the Voting Rights Act of 1965—and a way of appealing to the conscience of right-minded citizens everywhere. Civil disobedience as a way of protest involved the right of citizens to disobey laws they considered morally wrong. Arrests were expected and accepted; King was arrested scores of times and served several jail sentences with hundreds of his followers.

Nonviolent direct action was intended to dramatize the plight of the Negro, to bring recognition of his legally guaranteed rights, and to force the legal action needed to bring them to reality. The techniques used were many—public demonstrations of all sorts, freedom rides, freedom and prayer marches and vigils, sit-ins, kneel-ins, lie-downs, and boycotts. The nonviolent protest movement directly resulted in at least twelve murders. Beatings and physical violence were common.

After the Montgomery victory, the movement spread rapidly, and in 1964 King was awarded the Nobel Peace Prize. In this first decade of the civil-rights struggle, he was the recognized leader of his race as head of the Southern Christian Leadership Conference, and his followers took courage from his dedication.

A sniper's bullet struck King in Memphis, Tennessee, on April 4, 1968. He had gone to the city to assist the members of the sanitation men's union to be recognized as an established municipal union. He was on the balcony of a motel that afternoon when a single rifle shot aimed from the window of a nearby rooming house smashed his neck, exploded against his lower right jaw, severed his spinal cord, and slammed him against a wall. He died within an hour.

Concentrated police and Federal Bureau of Investigation inquiry led authorities to suspect a man named James Earl Ray as the murderer. The search, which followed Ray to Canada and England, ended when, by a strange coincidence, he was captured on the same day that Senator Kennedy was assassinated.

Ray's record was one of poverty, rootlessness, and shiftlessness. An escaped convict, a loner, a discharged soldier, and a Negro hater, he is generally thought to have been a hired killer, but details of the conspiracy, if there was one, are yet to be revealed.

The murder of Dr. King was in every way a catastrophe.

It touched off a black rampage that subjected the United States to the most widespread spasm of disorder in its violent history. Civil disorders ranging from large-scale riots to random shopwindow breaking struck more than 130 cities, causing $45 million worth of damage to insured property alone and accounting for more than twenty thousand arrests and countless injuries. Considering the scope of the disorders, however, the number of deaths—thirty-nine—was mercifully small. The creed of nonviolence which King had sponsored has since been challenged by the activities of black militants. His death left a void which may never be filled. King's assassin, James Earl Ray, was sentenced to ninety-nine years in prison in April, 1969.

Assassination—an ugly, hissing word for an ugly act—is indeed "a special kind of murder." It is a kind of murder, heinous, as all murder, for its violent brutality, but doubly heinous in this aspect: that it denies to every citizen except the assassin the right to make his own decision, to accept or reject, by his vote, the programs espoused by the murdered leader. The assassin alone, by his act, decides these questions for an entire nation.

It is a kind of murder that may destroy much more—many lives and hopes and dreams—than the crazed killer intends; for the death of a leader irrevocably alters the course of history, and in that alteration much that is good, much that is hopeful and humanitarian may be lost forever. It is, in that sense, an assault on every man and on men and nations yet unborn.

APPENDIX

OTHER MAJOR ASSASSINATIONS

336 B.C. Philip II, King of Macedon, father of Alexander the Great, stabbed by one of his soldiers.
1537 Alessandro de' Medici, First Duke of Florence, stabbed by an assassin hired by Lorenzino de' Medici, his cousin.
1546 Cardinal David Beaton, Scottish churchman, by a Protestant reformer.
1547 Lorenzino de' Medici, by an assassin hired by his cousin, Cosimo de' Medici (see above).
1584 William I, Prince of Orange ("The Silent"), by a French Catholic fanatic.
1589 Henry III, King of France, by a monk.
1610 Henry IV, King of France, stabbed by a Roman Catholic fanatic.

1628 George Villiers, First Duke of Buckingham, stabbed by a discontented naval officer.
1634 General Albrecht von Wallenstein, Austrian General, murdered by a band of his officers.
1679 Archbishop James Sharp, Scottish churchman, murdered by a group of opposition Covenanters (a previous attempt unsuccessful).
1792 Gustavus III, King of Sweden, by a representative of the nobles.
1800 Jean Kléber, French General, by a Muslim fanatic in Cairo.
1801 Paul I, Czar of Russia, son of Catherine the Great, strangled by conspirators.
1808 Selim III, Sultan of Turkey, strangled by a member of the military class.
1810 Count Axel Fersen, Swedish Marshal and friend of French Queen Marie Antoinette, killed by a mob.
1819 August Friedrich von Kotzebue, agent of the Russian Czar, stabbed by a university student in Mannheim, Germany.
1820 Charles Ferdinand, Duc de Berry, French heir apparent, stabbed by a member of the opposition.
1829 Aleksandr Griboyedov, Russian Ambassador to Persia, murdered with members of the embassy staff in Teheran by a mob.
1831 Ionnes Capidostrias, First President of Greece, assassinated by the son and brother of an imprisoned leader of the opposition.
1848 Count Pellegrino Luigi Rossi, Prime Minister of the Papal States, by extremists.
1860 Danilo II, Prince of Montenegro, by a Montenegrin exile.
1862 General Santos Guardiola, President of Honduras.
1868 Michael Obrenović, Prince of Serbia, by members of a rival family.
1870 Marshal Juan Prim, Prime Minister of Spain, by political enemies.
1871 Georges Darboy, Archbishop of Paris, shot by Communards while in prison during the siege of Paris.
1875 Gabriel García Moreno, President of Ecuador, stabbed with a machete by a group of anti-Catholics.
1876 Abdul-Aziz, Sultan of Turkey, murdered in prison.
1876 Hussein Avni, Turkish Minister of Foreign Affairs, shot by a member of the staff of Abdul Aziz (see above).
1882 Lord Frederick Cavendish, British Chief Secretary for Ireland,

OTHER MAJOR ASSASSINATIONS

killed together with Under-Secretary Thomas Burke, by members of the Irish Invincibles in Dublin.

1882 Mehemet Ali Pasha, Turkish General, mobbed and killed by insurgents in Albania.

1894 Marie Sadi Carnot, President of France, stabbed by an Italian anarchist.

1896 Juan Idiarte Borda, President of Uruguay.

1897 Antonio Cánovas del Castillo, Prime Minister of Spain, by an Italian anarchist.

1898 Elizabeth, Empress of Austria and Queen of Hungary, wife of Emperor Francis Joseph, stabbed by an Italian anarchist in Geneva, Switzerland.

1900 Humbert (Umberto) I, King of Italy, shot by an anarchist who had come from the United States (two previous attempts unsuccessful).

1903 Alexander Obrenović, King of Serbia, and his wife, Queen Draga, by a group of army officers.

1908 Carlos I, King of Portugal, and his son, Crown Prince Luis Felipe.

1910 Butrus Pasha Ghali, Prime Minister of Egypt.

1912 José Canalejas y Méndez, Prime Minister of Spain, by an anarchist.

1913 George I, King of Greece, shot a few days before the fiftieth anniversary of his accession.

1913 Nazim Pasha, Minister of War of Turkey and Commander-in-Chief of the Turkish Army.

1913 Shevket Pasha, Grand Vizier of Turkey, by nationalists.

1933 Ion Duca, Prime Minister of Rumania.

1934 Bronislaw Pieracki, Polish Minister of the Interior, by Ukrainian terrorists.

1934 Engelbert Dollfuss, Chancellor of Austria, by an Austrian Nazi.

1934 Alexander I, King of Yugoslavia, and Jean Louis Barthou, Foreign Minister of France, both shot by a Croatian terrorist at Marseilles while they were on a state visit to France.

1942 Jean François Darlan, French Admiral, by a French anti-fascist.

1964 Jigme Dorji, Premier of Bhutan, shot by a soldier.

SELECTED READING

For assassinations of the past, accounts of varying lengths may be found in biographies and many country and period histories. Those consulted for the writing of this book are too numerous to be listed, and only the principal and more readily available sources for the major assassinations are listed below.

Chapter 1 Murder for a Cause

BUCKLEY, WILLIAM F., JR. "The Politics of Assassination." *Esquire,* Vol. 70 (October 1968), pp. 163–65, 228–30, 234, 236.

DEDIJER, VLADIMIR. *The Road to Sarajevo.* Simon and Schuster,

1966. pp. 19–26; Appendix, Major Political Assassinations, 1792–1914, pp. 449–51.

HERBERG, WILL. "Political Assassination: Two Historical Types." *National Review,* Vol. 20 (July 2, 1968), pp. 656, 669.

LEWIS, BERNARD. *The Assassins: A Radical Sect in Islam.* Basic Books, 1968.

SPARROW, GERALD. *The Great Assassins.* Arco, 1969.

Two recent books published in Great Britain are:

GRIBBLE, LEONARD R. *Hands of Terror: Notable Assassinations of the Twentieth Century.* F. Muller, 1960.

WILLIAMS, JOHN. *Heyday for Assassins.* Heineman, 1958.

Chapter 2 Assassins and Their Plots

LEVINE, ISAAC DON. *The Mind of an Assassin.* Farrar, Straus, and Cudahy, 1959.

ROSENBERG, CHARLES E. *The Trial of the Assassin, Guiteau.* University of Chicago Press, 1968.

Those sources listed under Chapter 15 also contain material relevant to this chapter.

Chapter 3 Two Biblical Assassinations

The major sources are in the Old Testament book of Judges, as cited. Bible commentaries and source books offer added information.

Chapter 4 Daggers and Swords in Ancient Rome

Major biographies of Caesar and Cicero include somewhat detailed accounts. Plutarch's *Lives* and Shakespeare's *Julius Caesar* are best for Caesar.

Chapter 5 Murder in a Cathedral

DUGGAN, ALFRED. *My Life for my Sheep.* Coward-McCann, 1955. pp. 313–37.

ELIOT, T. S. *Murder in the Cathedral.* Harcourt, 1935. Drama.

WINSTON, RICHARD. *Thomas Becket.* Knopf, 1967. pp. 351–66.

Chapter 6 A Crusader-Victim of the Hashasheen

Brief mention is made in general histories of the Crusades and specialized books on the Third Crusade.

LEWIS, BERNARD. *The Assassins.* Basic Books, 1968. pp. 98–99, 102–3.

Chapter 7 A Leader of the French Revolution

The most authoritative accounts are to be found in the standard books on the French Revolution, especially that of Thomas Carlyle (1837), and biographies of Corday and Marat.

FISHER, JOHN. *Six Summers in Paris, 1789–1794.* Harper, 1966. pp. 155–56.

WEISS, PETER. *Persecution and Assassination of John-Paul Marat as Performed by the Inmates of the Asylum of Charenton . . .* Atheneum, 1965. Drama.

Chapter 8 The Fuse of World War I: Sarajevo

DEDIJER, VLADIMIR. *The Road to Sarajevo.* Simon and Schuster, 1966. pp. 9–26.

FEUERLICHT, ROBERTA S. *The Desperate Act.* McGraw-Hill, 1968.

MASSIE, ROBERT K. *Nicholas and Alexandra.* Atheneum, 1967. pp. 253–57.

Chapter 9 Victims of the Russian Revolution

Nicholas II and His Family

MASSIE, ROBERT K. *Nicholas and Alexandra.* Atheneum, 1967. pp. 490–98.

Rasputin

MASSIE, ROBERT K. *Nicholas and Alexandra.* Atheneum, 1967. pp. 372–83.

WILSON, COLIN. *Rasputin and the Fall of the Romanovs.* Citadel, 1967 (paperback). pp. 190–95.

Trotsky

LEVINE, ISAAC DON. *The Mind of the Assassin.* Farrar, Straus, and Cudahy, 1959.
Life, Vol. 9 (September 2, 1940), pp. 17–21.
Newsweek, Vol. 16 (September 2, 1940), p. 23.
Time, Vol. 36 (September 2, 1950), pp. 21–22; (September 9, 1950), p. 32.

Chapter 10 Violent Death of a Nonviolent Leader

ASHE, GEOFFREY. *Gandhi.* Stein and Day, 1968. pp. 375–85.
FISCHER, LOUIS. *The Life of Mahatma Gandhi.* Harper, 1950. pp. 502–5.
Life, Vol. 24 (February 9, 1948), pp. 27–31.
Newsweek, Vol. 31 (February 9, 1948), pp. 24–26.
Time, Vol. 51 (February 9, 1948), pp. 24–26; (June 7, 1948), p. 33 (trial).
WOLPERT, STANLEY. *Nine Hours to Rama.* Random House, 1962. Fiction.

Chapters 11 to 14

Some information on the assassinations in these areas and countries may be found in general political histories. For the more modern, post-World War II murders, full contemporary accounts may be found in *Facts on File* and periodicals such as *Life, Newsweek, Senior Scholastic, Time,* and *U.S. News and World Report.* References to such articles may be located in *Readers Guide* issues near the date of the assassinations under either the name of the country or the person murdered. Background material may be found in up-to-date political histories.

Chapter 15 Guns in the United States

PRESIDENTS

Accounts of attempts and successful assassinations are numerous and include full-length books as well as individual biographies.

SELECTED READING

BROOKS, STEWART M. *Our Murdered Presidents: The Medical Story.* Fell, 1965.
DONOVAN, ROBERT J. *The Assassins.* Harper, 1955.
POTTER, JOHN M. *Plots against Presidents.* Astor-Honor, 1967.

A 1968 study of American presidential assassins has been prepared by the staff of the National Advisory Commission on Civil Disorders, but is not generally available.

Comments on Recent Assassinations, 1963–1968
FRANKEL, CHARLES. "The Meaning of Political Murder." *Saturday Review,* Vol. 51 (June 22, 1968), pp. 17–18.
"Politics and Assassination; Time Essay." *Time,* Vol. 91 (June 14, 1968), p. 91.
"Question of Value: Death Penalty in Case of Assassination of President or Vice President." *Time,* Vol. 86 (July 2, 1965), pp. 16–17.
"U.S. Guilt in Assassinations, the Talk and the Facts." *U.S. News and World Report,* Vol. 64 (June 24, 1968), p. 37.

Studies of Recent Assassins, 1963–1968
HARTOGS, RENATUS, and LUCY FREEMAN. *The Two Assassins.* Crowell, 1965.
LINN, EDWARD. "The Next Assassin." *True,* Vol. 49 (November 1968), pp. 25–29, 69–73.
O'NEIL, PAUL. "Ray, Sirhan: What Possessed Them?" *Life,* Vol. 64 (June 21, 1968), pp. 24–34.

John F. Kennedy
BISHOP, JIM. *The Day Kennedy Was Shot.* Funk and Wagnalls, 1968.
Life, Vol. 55 (November 29, 1963), pp. 22–32.
Newsweek, Vol. 62 (December 2, 1963), pp. 20–26; Vol. 64 (December 4, 1964), pp. 28–30.
President's Commission on the Assassination of President Kennedy. *Report* (The Warren Report). Government Printing

Office and Doubleday, 1964. Paperback, Bantam, 1964.
Time, Vol. 82 (November 29, 1963), pp. 21–27; abridged in *Readers Digest,* Vol. 84 (January 1964), pp. 39–44.
U.S. News and World Report, Vol. 57 (December 7, 1964), pp. 68–70.

SENATORS
Huey Long
DEUTSCH, HERMANN B. *The Huey Long Case.* Doubleday, 1963.
New Republic, Vol. 85 (January 1, 1936), pp. 215–18.
Newsweek, Vol. 6 (September 14, 1935), pp. 5–6.
Time, Vol. 26 (September 16, 1935), p. 15.
ZINMAS, DAVID H. *The Day Huey Long Was Shot, September 8, 1935.* Obolensky, 1963.

Robert F. Kennedy
Assassination: Robert F. Kennedy, 1925–1968, by the editors of United Press International. Cowles, 1968.
Life, Vol. 64 (June 14, 1968), pp. 32–42.
Newsweek, Vol. 71 (June 17, 1968), pp. 20–40.
New Yorker, Vol. 44 (June 15, 1968), pp. 90–96.
Time, Vol. 91 (June 14, 1968), pp. 15–18.
U.S. News and World Report, Vol. 64 (June 17, 1968), pp. 16–18, 25–28, 99.

MAYORS
Anton Cermak
Christian Century, Vol. 50 (March 15, 1933), pp. 347–48.
GOTTFRIED, ALEX. *Boss Cermak of Chicago.* University of Washington Press, 1962. pp. 328–31.
Literary Digest, Vol. 115 (March 18, 1933), pp. 26–28.

CIVIL-RIGHTS LEADER
Martin Luther King, Jr.
Life, Vol. 64 (April 19, 1968), pp. 28–33.
Newsweek, Vol. 71 (April 15, 1968), pp. 34–38; Vol. 71 (June 24, 1968), p. 32.
Time, Vol. 91 (April 12, 1968), pp. 18–21.

INDEX

Last names of assassination victims are capitalized, with date in parentheses

ABDUL-AZIZ, Sultan of Turkey (1876), 204
ABDULLAH, King of Jordan (1951), 104, 105, 107, 108
Aden, 4
Africa, 156–157; assassinations, 21, 157–68 (*see also* Algeria; Burundi; Congo; Togo; Union of South Africa); attempts, 158, 160, 164–165; protection of political leaders, 18
Aizawa, Col. Sabuto, 122
ALEKSANDROV, Todor, Bulgarian Prime Minister (1924), 8
ALEXANDER I, King of Yugoslavia, (1934), 205
ALEXANDER II, Czar of Russia (1881), 74
ALEXANDRA, Czarina of Russia (1918), 74–77, 78–79, 83–84; Rasputin and, 75, 80–81
ALEXIS, Czarevitch of Russia (1918), 76, 78–79, 80–81
Algeria, 157; assassination, 158; attempts, 158
AMIN-ES-SULTAN, Persian Premier (1907), 33, 98
anarchists, 28–29; Russian, 6–7, 21, 73, 74–75
ANASTASIA, Grand Duchess of Russia (1918), 78–79
Antony, Mark, 45–46, 47, 48
Aqa, Abbas, 33, 98–99
Arab-Jewish conflict, 96, 101, 104–105, 107, 109–110, 112–113, 114–115
ARANA, Francisco, Guatemalan General (1949), 136–137
Arbenz, Jacobo, President of Guatemala, 136–137
ARINORI, Mori, Japanese Minister of Education (1885), 120–121
ASANUMA, Inejiro, Japanese politician (1960), 124–125
Asia: protection of political leaders, 18
Asia, southern, 116–117; assassinations, 125–130 (*see also* Ceylon; Laos; Vietnam, Republic of)
assassin: derivation of word, 4, 57, 96
assassinate: definitions of word, 4–5
assassination: elements in, 23–29; historical overview of, 6–10; "magnicide," 33, 150; major, not included in text, list, 203–205; place element, 24–28; plots, 20–35; protection of modern heads of state, 17–19, 185–188, 191; recognition of murderer, 29; regicide, 10–11, 21; successful, results of, 31–32; surprise in, 29; time element, 23–24; as a type of murder, 10–19, 201; types, 14–16; tyrannicide, 15–16, 21, 44, 134
assassination attempts, 16–17; April 1968–January 1969, 4; unsuccessful, results of, 29–31

assassins: characteristics, 32–36; dedication of, 6–7, 8, 14, 15, 16, 18, 33–34, 98–99, 107, 112, 119–120, 121, 123–124, 125, 191; disappointed office seekers, 14–15, 178; group conspiracies, 20–23; mental disorders of, 15, 16, 32, 33, 170, 178–179, 180–181; plots, 20–35; purpose, 23; revolt against national or colonial leadership, 15; weapons used, 28–29
Austria: assassinations in, 205
Austro-Hungarian Empire, 21, 67; assassinations, 66–71, 204, 205
AVNI, Hussein, Turkish Minister of Foreign Affairs (1876), 204

Balkans: assassinations, 8–9, 28, 66–71, 204, 205
Bandaranaike, Mrs. Sirimavo, 118
BANDARANAIKE, Solomon, Ceylonese Prime Minister (1959), 27, 117–118
al-BANNA, Sheikh Hassan (1949), 108
BARRIOS, José, President of Guatemala (1898), 136
BARTHOU, Jean Louis, French Foreign Minister (1934), 205
BEATON, Cardinal David (1546), 203
BECKET, Thomas à, Archbishop of Canterbury (1170), 29, 49–55
Begley, Col. Frank, 114
Bellingham, John, 27
Ben Bella, Algerian leader: attempts on life, 158
BERNADOTTE, Count Folke, United Nations Mediator for Palestine (1948), 22, 107, 112–114
BERRY (or BERRI), Charles Ferdinand, Duc de (1820), 204
Betancourt, Rómulo, President of Venezuela: attempt on life, 154–155
Bhutan: assassination in, 205
Bible: assassinations in, 36–42
Biha, Leopold, Burundi Premier: attempt on life, 160
BOGOLEPOV, Nikolai, Russian Minister of Education (1901), 74
Bolivia: assassinations in, 132
Bolsheviks, 73, 76–78, 79, 82–83
bombs: use of by assassins, 28–29
Booth, John Wilkes, 15, 175–176, 177
Bosnia, 66–67
Brezhnev, Leonid, Communist leader: attempt on life, 7–8
Brown, George, 9
Brutus, Marcus, 29, 44–45
Bulgaria: assassinations, 8–9
BURKE, Thomas, British official in Ireland (1882), 10, 204–205
Burundi, 158–159; assassination, 159–160

CACERES, Ramón, President of Dominican Republic (1911), 133

INDEX

CAESAR, Julius (44 B. C.), 16, 29, 43–46
Canada: assassination in, 9, 26–27
CANALEJAS Y MÉNDEZ, José, Spanish Prime Minister (1912), 205
CÁNOVAS DEL CASTILLO, Antonio, Spanish Prime Minister (1897), 205
CAPIDOSTRAS, Ionnes, President of Greece (1831), 204
Caribbean area, 131–132; assassinations, 132; (*see also* Dominican Republic)
CARLOS I, King of Portugal (1908), 205
CARNOT, Marie Sadi, President of France (1894), 205
CARRANZA, Venustiano, President of Mexico (1920), 143–144
CASTILLO ARMAS, Col. Carlos, President of Guatemala (1957), 137–138
CAVENDISH, Lord Frederick, British official in Ireland (1882), 10, 204–205
Central America, 131; (*see also* Guatemala; Honduras; Mexico; Nicaragua; Panama)
CERMAK, Anton, Mayor of Chicago (1933), 173, 195–197
Ceylon: assassination, 27, 117–118
CHAMOUN, Camille, Ex-President of Lebanon (1968), 109
CHOTEK, Countess Sophie (1914), 28, 67–71
CICERO, Marcus Tullius (43 B. C.), 16, 46–48
civil disobedience: of Gandhi, 91–92; of King, 197–198
Collazo, Oscar, 172–174
Communists, 6, 7, 73, 84, 86–87, 103, 104, 119, 123, 125–127, 136, 137–138, 159–160, 183–184
Congo, Democratic Republic of, 161; assassinations, 162–163
Connally, John B., Jr., 182
CONRAD OF MONTFERRAT (1192), 6, 57–59
Corday, Charlotte, 62–64
Cosa Nostra, 13–14
Crusaders and Crusades, 6, 56–59
Czolgosz, Leon, 15, 180–181

DANILO II, Prince of Montenegro (1860), 204
DARBOY, Georges, Archbishop of Paris (1871), 204
DARLAN, Jean François, French Admiral (1942), 205
Darnley, Lord (Henry Stuart), 11
Deborah, 39, 41
Dediger, Vladimir; *The Road to Sarajevo*, quoted, 72
de Gaulle, Charles, President of France: attempts on life, 18
DELGADO CHALBAUD, Carlos, President of Venezuela (1950), 153–154
Diaz, Gen. Juan, 135–136
Díaz, Porfirio, 139
Dictators, 22, 131–132, 133–136, 139, 153, 155
DIEM, Ngo Dinh, President of South Vietnam (1963), 127–128
Dirksen, Everett, 187
DOLLFUSS, Engelbert, Chancellor of Austria (1934), 205

Dominican Republic, 131, 133; assassinations, 132, 133–136
DORJI, Jigme, Bhutan Premier (1964), 205
DRAGA, Queen of Serbia (1903), 205
DUCA, Ion, Rumanian Prime Minister (1933), 205

Ecuador: assassination, 204
Edward V, King of England: murder (1483), 11–12
EGLON, King of Moab (c. 1200 B. C.), 37–39
Egypt: assassinations, 107–108, 205
Ehud the Benjamite, 37–39
Eisenhower, Dwight D., U.S. President, 150, 187
El Fatah: *see* Fatah
ELIZABETH, Empress of Austria and Queen of Hungary (1898), 205
EL NOKRASHY, Mahmoud Fahmy: *see* NOKRASHY
Europe: assassinations in, 4; (*see also* countries of Europe)

FAISAL II, King of Iraq (1958), 100–101
Far East, 116–117; *see also* Japan; Philippines
Fatah, El Fatah, 22–23
FERSEN, Count Axel, Swedish Marshal (1810), 205
Fitzurse, Reginald, 53–54
Forty-Seven Ronin, 119–120
France: assassinations, 4, 60–65, 203, 204, 205; protection of President, 18
FRANZ FERDINAND, Archduke of Austria-Hungary (1914), 28, 67–71
French Revolution, 60–65
FULLER, Lance Corporal Arthur (1945), 111

Gallagher, James J., 193–194
GANDHI, Mohandas (Mahatma) (1948), 27, 89–92, 93–94; attempt on life, 93
GARCÍA MORENO, Gabriel, President of Ecuador (1875), 204
GARFIELD, James A., U.S. President (1881), 14, 15, 171, 177–179, 185
Gaynor, William, Mayor of New York City: attempt on life, 194
GEORGE I, King of Greece (1913), 205
GEORGIEV, Kosta, Bulgarian General (1925), 9
GHALI, Butrus Pasha, Egyptian Prime Minister (1910), 205
Godse, Nathuram, 93
GOEBEL, William, Governor of Kentucky (1900), 191–193
Great Britain: assassinations, 9–10, 14, 27, 49–55; attempts, 16–17; protection of Prime Minister, 17
Greece: assassinations, 16, 204, 205; attempts, 4
Grey, Sir Edward: quoted, 72
GRIBOYEDOV, Aleksandr, Russian Ambassador to Persia (1829), 204
GUARDIOLA, Gen. Santos, President of Honduras (1862), 204
Guatemala: assassinations: 136–139
Guinness, Walter E., *see* Moyne, Lord

Guiteau, Charles, 15, 178–179
Guizado, José, 153
Guns: use of by assassins, 28, 29
GUSTAVUS III, King of Sweden (1792), 204

Hakim, Eliahu, 111–112
HAMAGUCHI, Osachi, Japanese Prime Minister (1930), 122
HARRISON, Carter, Mayor of Chicago (1893), 15, 25, 194–196
Hasan ibn-al Sabbah (Old Man of the Mountain), 5, 98
Hashasheen, Islami sect, 4–5, 34, 57–59, 96, 98, 107
Heber the Canaanite, 40, 41
Henry II, King of England, 49–50, 51, 55
HENRY III, King of France (1589), 203
HENRY IV, King of France (1610), 203
HEUREAUX, Ulises, President of Dominican Republic (1899), 133
HEYDRICH, Reinhard (1942), 31–32
HIROBUMI, Prince Ito, Japanese Prime Minister (1909), 121
Hirohito, Emperor of Japan: attempt on life, 4
Hitler, Adolf: attempt on life, 29–31
Honduras: assassination, 204
Hughes-Onslow, Capt. Arthur, 111
HUMBERT I, King of Italy (1900), 205
Huong, Tran Van, South Vietnam Premier: attempt on life, 130
Hussein, King of Jordan: attempts on life, 105–106

IDIARTE BORDA, Juna, President of Uruguay (1896), 205
ILLAH, Abdul, Crown Prince of Iraq, (1958), 100–101
India: assassination in, 21, 89–94
Iran, 95; assassinations, 99–100; see also Persia
Iraq: assassinations, 100–104; military coup, 101–103
Ireland: assassinations, 3, 10
Irgun (National Military Organization), 22, 109–110
Israel: assassinations, 113–115; see also Palestine
Italy: assassinations, 203, 205

Jackson, Andrew, U.S. President: attempt on life, 170–171
Jacson (or Jackson), Frank, see Mercader, Ramón
Jael, 40–41
Japan: assassinations, 3, 8, 15, 120–125; attempts, 4, 122–123; dedication of assassins, 8, 119–120, 121, 123–124, 125
Johnson, Andrew, U. S. Vice President, 176, 177
Johnson, Lyndon B., 128, 182, 187
Jordan, Hashemite Kingdom of, 95; assassinations, 105–107; attempt, 106
Judges, Book of, 36–37, 38–41

Kasavubu, Joseph, 162
KASSEM, Abdul Karim, Iraqi General (1963), 101, 103–104
Keisuke, Okada, Japanese Premier: attempt on life, 122–123

Kennedy, Edward, 187
KENNEDY, John F., U. S. President (1963), 24, 169, 181–185, 187; Warren Commission Report, 184–185, 186
KENNEDY, Robert F., U. S. Senator (1968), 4, 34, 169, 186, 189–191
Khan, Mohammed Ayub, President of Pakistan: attempt on life, 4
KHEMISTI, Mohammed, Algerian Foreign Minister (1963), 158
Khruschev, Nikita, Soviet Premier: attempts on life, 7
KING, Martin Luther, Jr., Negro civil rights leader (1968), 4, 13, 169, 197–199
KIROV, Sergei, Communist leader (1934), 6
KLÉBER, Jean, French General (1800), 204
KOREKIGO, Takahashi, Japanese Minister of Finance (1936), 123
KOTZEBUE, August Friedrich von, Russian agent (1819), 204

Laos: assassination, 125–126
Latin America, 131–132; assassinations, 4, 132, 135–155 (see also Ecuador; Guatemala; Honduras; Mexico; Nicaragua; Panama; Uruguay; Venezuela); attempts, 146, 154–55; protection of political leaders, 18–19; terrorist groups, 22, 136–37, 145
Lawrence, Richard, 170
Lebanon: assassinations, 4, 108–109
Lenin, Vladimir, 6, 77, 82, 84
LINCOLN, Abraham, U. S. President (1865), 15, 171, 175–77, 185; attempt on life, 171
LONG, Huey, U. S. Senator (1935), 188, 189
LUMUMBA, Patrice, Congolese Premier (1961), 162–163

McGEE, Darcy, Canadian Parliament member (1868), 9, 26–27
MCKINLEY, William, U. S. President (1901), 15, 171, 179–181, 185
MacMichael, Sir Harold, British official: attempt on life, 110
MADERO, Francisco, President of Mexico (1913), 140–142
Mafia, 13–14
"magnicide," 33, 150
MAJALI, Hazzah, Jordanian Premier (1960), 106
Malcolm X: murder (1965), 13
MANSOUR, Hassan Ali, Iranian Premier (1965), 97, 99–100
MARAT, Jean-Paul, leader in French Revolution (1793), 61–64
MARIE, Grand Duchess of Russia (1918), 78–79
Mary Stuart, Queen of Scots, 11–12
MASUJIRO, Omura, Japanese Minister of Military Affairs (1869), 120
MAYO, Earl of (Richard Bourke) (1872), 33, 90–91
MEDICI, Alessandro de' (1537), 203
MEDICI, Lorenzino de' (1548), 203
MEHEMET ALI PASHA, Turkish General (1882), 205
MEIN, John, U. S. Ambassador to Guatemala (1968), 4, 9, 138–139

INDEX

Mercader, Ramón, 86–88
Mesopotamia, 95, 100, 109; (see also Iraq)
Mexico: assassinations, 140–149; Revolution, 139–40, 143
MICHAEL, Grand Duke of Russia (1918), 76–77, 79
Middle East, 95–96, 107; assassinations, 4, 9, 10, 18, 24, 33–34, 96–115; (see also Egypt; Iran; Israel; Jordan; Lebanon; Palestine; Persia; Syria); dedication of assassins, 6–7, 15, 18, 33–34, 98–99, 107, 112, 191; protection of political leaders, 18; terrorist groups, 22–23, 96, 101–102, 107–108; (see also Irgun; Stern Gang)
MIRBACH, Count Wilhelm von, German Ambassador to Russia (1918), 77
Miró, Rubén, 152
Monarchies: conspiracies against rulers, 10–12, 21; fall of, 6, 12, 21, 22, 73–79
MORAY, Earl of (Lord James Stuart) (1570), 11–12
MOYNE, Lord (Walter Edward Guinness), British Minister of State in Middle East) (1944), 10, 22, 27, 110–112
MPOLO, Maurice, Congolese Youth Minister (1961), 162–163
Muslim Brothers, 107–108
Mussafer-ed-Din, Shah of Persia: attempt on life, 98

NAOSUKE, Ii, Japanese Prime Minister (1860), 120
NASR-ED-DIN, Shah of Persia (1896), 97–98
Nasser, Gamal Abdel, 103, 104; attempt on life, 108
nationalism and nationalists, 10, 21–22, 101, 120–124
NAZIM PASHA, Turkish Minister of War (1913), 205
Netherlands: Assassination, 203
NGENDANDUMWE, Pierre, Burundi Prime Minister (1965), 159–160
NHU, Ngo Dinh, South Vietnamese Chief of Police (1963), 127–128
Nicaragua, 149; assassination, 149–150
NICHOLAS II, Czar of Russia (1918), 12, 73–79, 83–84
Nixon, Richard M., U. S. President, 186–187, 188
Nokrashy, El Nokrashy, Mahmoud Fahmy, Egyptian Premier (1948), 107–108
NURI-ES-SAID, Iraqi Premier (1958), 101, 102–103

OBREGÓN, Alvaro, President of Mexico (1928), 140, 143, 144, 147–149
OBRENOVIĆ, Alexander, King of Serbia (1903), 205
OBRENOVIĆ, Michael, Prince of Serbia (1868), 204
OKITO, Joseph, Congolese Senate Vice President (1961), 162–163
OLGA, Grand Duchess of Russia (1918), 78–79
OLYMPIO, Sylvanus, President of Togo (1963), 165–166

Oswald, Lee Harvey, 24, 183–184

Pahlevi, Mohammed Reza, Shah of Iran, 96–97, 99–100; attempts on life, 97
Paine, Lewis, 176–177
Pakistan: assassination attempt, 4
Palestine, 95, 104, 109–110; assassinations, 96, 109–112; terrorist groups in, 22 (see also Irgun; Stern Gang); (see also Israel)
Panama, 151; assassinations, 151–153
Papadapoulos, George, Greek Premier: attempt on life, 4
Pathet Lao, 125–126
PAUL I, Czar of Russia (1801), 12, 204
PERCEVAL, Spencer, British Prime Minister (1812), 10, 14
Persia, 95; assassinations, 97–98; (see also Iran)
PHILIP II, King of Macedon (336 B. C.), 203
Philippines: assassination, 4
PIERACKI, Bronislaw, Polish Minister of Interior (1934), 205
PINO SUÁREZ, José María, Vice President of Mexico (1913), 141–142
PLEHVE, Vyacheslav, Russian Minister of Interior (1904), 75
Pobiedonotsev, Constantine, 75
Podgorny, Nikolai, President of Soviet Union: attempt on life, 7–8
Poland: assassination, 205
Portugal: assassinations, 205
Powers, Caleb, 192–193
Pratt, David, 34, 165
PRIM, Marshal Juan, Spanish Prime Minister (1870), 204
Princip, Gavrilo, 28, 69–71

QUINIM PHOLSENA, Laos Foreign Minister (1963), 125–126

RASPUTIN, Gregory (1916), 12, 25, 79–82; attempts on life, 81
Ray, James Earl, 198–199
RAZMARA, ALI, Iranian Premier (1951), 99
Regicide, 10–11, 21
REMÓN CANTERA, José, President of Panama (1955), 151–152
Richard III, King of England, 11–12
Rizzio, David, 11
Rockwell, George Lincoln: murder (1967), 13
Romanov dynasty, 12, 72, 73–79, 83–84
Rome: assassinations, 3, 16, 29, 43–48
Roosevelt, Franklin D., U. S. President: attempt on life, 172–173, 195–196
Roosevelt, Theodore, U. S. President, 185; attempt on life, 171–172
ROSSI, Count Pellegrino Luigi, Papal States Prime Minister (1848), 204
Ruby, Jack, 183–184
Rumania: assassination, 205
Russia: anarchists in, 6–7, 22, 73, 74–75; assassinations, 6, 12, 74–82, 204; attempts, 7–8, 74, 75, 81; 1917 Revolution, 76–77, 82–83; terrorist groups, 22, 73, 74–75; (see also Union of Soviet Socialist Republics)
RWANGASORE, Louis, Burundi Prince and Premier (1961), 159

INDEX

SAITO, Makoto, Japanese Admiral (1936), 123
Saladin: attempt on life, 58
Sánchez, Guadalupe, 143–144
Sarajevo: assassination of Archduke Franz Ferdinand and wife (1914), 9, 28, 66–71; results, 71–72
Schrank, John M., 172
Scotland: assassinations, 203, 204
SELIM III, Sultan of Turkey (1808), 204
Serbia: assassinations, 204, 205
SERGE, Grand Duke of Russia (1905), 74
SEROT, Col. André (1948), 114
Seward, William, U. S. Secretary of State: attempt on life, 176–177
SHARP, James, Scottish Archbishop (1679), 204
Sheridan, John S., 9
SHEVKET PASHA, Grand Vizier of Turkey (1913), 205
SIPIAGIN, Dimitri, Russian Minister of Interior (1902), 75
Siqueiros, David, 86
Sirhan, Sirhan, 34, 190–191
SISERA, Canaanite General (1150 B. C.), 39–41
SOH, Riad es-, Lebanese Premier (1951), 108–109
SOMOZA, Anastasio, President of Nicaragua (1956), 149–150
South Africa, see Union of South Africa
South America, see Latin America
Soviet Union, see Union of Soviet Socialist Republics
Spain: assassinations, 204, 205
Spiegel, John: quoted, 32–33
Stalin, Josef, 7, 83, 84, 85
STAMBOLINSKI, Aleksandr, Bulgarian Prime Minister (1923), 8
Stauffenberg, Col. Klaus von, 30–31
Stern Gang (Fighters for Freedom), 22, 23, 107, 110–112, 113–114
STOLYPIN, Peter, Russian Prime Minister (1911), 75
Surratt, John, 177
Sweden: assassinations, 204
Syria: assassination, 108

Tahmasabi, Khalil, 99
TAKASHI, Hara, Japanese Premier (1921), 121
TATIANA, Grand Duchess of Russia (1918), 78–79
Terrorists, 22; Balkan, 66–71; Latin America, 22, 136–137, 145; Middle East, 22–23, 96, 101–102, 107–108; Palestine, 22 (see also Irgun; Stern Gang); Russian, 22, 73, 74–75
TETSURAN, Nagata, Japanese General (1936), 122
Tippit, J. D., 183
Togo, 166; assassinations, 167–168
Torresola, Griselio, 173–174
TOSHIMICHI, Okubo, Japanese Premier (1878), 120
Transjordan, 95, 96, 104; (see also Jordan)
TRI, Le Minh, South Vietnamese Minister of Education (1969), 129–130

TROTSKY, Leon (1940), 27, 83–84, 86–88; attempt on life, 85–86
TRUJILLO MOLINA, Rafael, President of Dominican Republic (1961), 134–136, 155
Truman, Harry, U. S. President, 187; attempt on life, 173–174
Tsafendas, Dimitrio, 166
Tshombe, Moise, 161, 163
TSUYOSHI, Inukai, Japanese Premier (1932), 122
Turkey: assassinations, 204, 205
Tyrannicide, 15–16, 21, 44, 134

Union of South Africa, 163–164; assassination, 165–166
Union of Soviet Socialist Republics, 7–8; protection of leaders, 8
United Nations, 112–113
United States: Ambassador, assassination, 4, 9, 138–139; assassinations, 4, 9, 12–13, 14–15, 32–33, 169–199; Governor, assassination, 191–193; Mayors, assassination, and attempts, 193–197; Presidents, assassination, 4, 9, 14, 15, 32–33, 169–170, 174–185; Presidents, attempts on lives, 9, 170–174; Presidents, protection of, 17, 185–188, 191; Senators, assassination, 188–191
Uruguay: assassination, 205

Venezuela, 153; assassination, 153–155
VERWOERD, Hendrik F., South African Prime Minister (1966), 165–166; attempt on life, 34, 164–165
Victoria, Queen of Great Britain, 75; attempts on life, 16–17
Vietnam, Republic of (South Vietnam): assassinations, 4, 127–130
VILLA, Francisco (Pancho), Mexican General and outlaw (1923), 143, 144–147
VILLIERS, George, Duke of Buckingham (1628), 204

WALLENSTEIN, Albrecht von, Austrian General (1634), 204
WASSON, Thomas, U. S. Consul in Jerusalem (1948), 9
WATANABE, Japanese General (1936), 123
Weiss, Carl, 189
Wertham, Frederic: quoted, 33
WILLIAM I, Prince of Orange (1584), 203
Wilson, Henry L., 141
World War I: Japan in, 121–122; Russia in, 76, 77, 80, 82–83; Sarajevo as cause, 71–72

Yakovlev, Vasily, 77
Yamaguchi, Otoya, 125
Yizernitsky, Itzhak, 23
Youssoupov, Felix, Russian Prince, 25, 81–82
Yugoslavia: assassination, 205
Yurovsky, Jacob, 78

ZAIM, Col. Husni, President of Syria (1949), 108
Zangara, Giuseppe, 172, 195–197
Zouri, Eliahu Bet, 111–112

8819